THE TEACHER'S GUIDE TO

Leading Student-Centered Discussions

We dedicate this book to Jack and Mary McCall, who insist that school is a place for students to engage their minds and hearts, and who show us that learning is not only a lifelong process, but is life itself.

THE TEACHER'S GUIDE TO

Leading Student-Centered Discussions

Talking About Texts in the Classroom

Michael S. Hale
Elizabeth A. City

CORWIN PRESS
A SAGE Publications Company
Thousand Oaks, California

For information:

Corwin Press
A Sage Publications Company
2455 Teller Road
Thousand Oaks, California 91320
www.corwinpress.com

Sage Publications Ltd.
1 Oliver's Yard
55 City Road
London EC1Y 1SP
United Kingdom

Sage Publications India Pvt. Ltd.
B-42, Panchsheel Enclave
Post Box 4109
New Delhi 110 017 India

Printed in the United States of America

Library of Congress Cataloging-in-Publication Data

Hale, Michael S.
The teacher's guide to leading student-centered discussions: Talking about texts in the classroom/Michael S. Hale, Elizabeth A. City.
    p. cm.
Includes bibliographical references and index.
ISBN 1-4129-0634-2 (cloth)—ISBN 1-4129-0635-0 (pbk.)
    1. Active learning. 2. Student-centered learning. 3. Discussion.
I. City, Elizabeth A. II. Title.
LB1027.23.H35 2006
371.37—dc22   2005031710

This book is printed on acid-free paper.

06   07   08   09   10   9   8   7   6   5   4   3   2   1

Acquisitions Editor:	Faye Zucker
Editorial Assistant:	Gem Rabanera
Production Editor:	Beth A. Bernstein
Copy Editor:	Jackie Tasch
Typesetter:	C&M Digitals (P) Ltd.
Proofreader:	Dennis W. Webb
Indexer:	Karen A. McKenzie
Cover Designer:	Rose Storey

Contents

Preface

"I think you are confusing *studies* with school. *Studies* can be gained from books and other places also," said Bethany to James. Sean added, "I agree with Bethany. If you look at the second to last sentence, he makes fun of *schoolmen*." The students in this European history class were engaged in a lively discussion of what they believed Francis Bacon meant by *studies* in his essay, "Of Studies." The text was dense and less accessible than much of what they had read in the past. After 20 minutes of swimming around the surface, they finally began to dive in. For the next 40 minutes they wrestled with ideas in the text, challenging and questioning the meaning of Bacon's words and their own ideas. The closing question—"What do you think Bacon would think of our schools today?"—yielded perhaps the most animated discussion of the day. Some students built arguments for Bacon being appalled at what they called our "focus on the superficial" whereas others suggested that he would be stunned that schools were open to everyone without regard to wealth or gender.

Later that day, Ms. Suarez, who had been facilitating, and Ms. O'Malley, who had been observing, reviewed the classroom conversation about "Of Studies." Ms. O'Malley was interested in having such conversations in her own classroom but had no experience with them, either as a teacher or as a student. Her questions came quickly, ranging from "Well, I don't think my students will listen to each other. How do I get them to listen?" to "What do you do if the conversation goes completely in a different direction than you planned?" Ms. Suarez answered each question, describing how she prepared for discussion and how she and the students had been working on their skills in different areas of discussion throughout the year. Ms. O'Malley responded, "Yes, I understand everything you're saying, but it seems like it's just instinct for you. It's not for me. What I want to know is how do you do that?"

We have worked with many teachers on leading discussions and have fielded the question of "But how do you do that?" many times. In this book, we will answer that question as completely as we can. This book is written for those who value collaborative inquiry, open-ended questions, and student-centered classroom discourse. Leading student-centered discussions is something that seems natural for some people and not so natural for other people. Like much of teaching, the role of the teacher in leading a discussion is more than simply following a set protocol or asking a series of questions. Also like much of teaching, leading a discussion can seem to fall somewhere between science, art, and magic, as the facilitator is faced with a constant stream of decisions based on ever-changing student behavior.

Part I of this book describes the science of leading a discussion: What are the basic elements of student-centered, text-based discussions, and how do you plan for such discussions? This section is designed for teachers who are new to this type of classroom discussion or for teachers who have been leading discussions by intuition. Part II delves into the art and magic of leading discussions: What is it that great facilitators do that makes them great, and how do you decide what to do during discussions as the conversation develops? Teachers already familiar with leading discussions might choose to start with this section. Part III offers numerous strategies to address the questions: What do you do when the discussion isn't going well, and how do you continue to improve as a facilitator?

In our experience as teachers, principals, and consultants, we have worked to improve our own facilitation, as well as to help other teachers learn to facilitate discussions. In this work, we have discovered that there are two distinct phases of learning to lead discussions. The first involves learning the fundamentals, which include choosing a text, writing questions, and setting up the classroom. These elements are mostly concrete and easy to grasp, although not necessarily easy to implement. The second and the most critical phase takes place once a teacher has gained some experience with these basic skills and activities. At this point, many facilitators continue to struggle to get students to have thoughtful, energetic, carefully considered conversations. Just as fishing is more than baiting the hook and casting, there is more to facilitating a discussion than basic skills. An expert fisherman knows where and when to cast, as well as what bait to use. Similarly, successful seminar facilitation is built on the excellent decision making of the facilitator.

As teachers who are interested in fostering stimulating dialogue in our own classrooms and the classrooms of others, we have tried to help teachers move beyond the basics and toward an understanding of how they can support students in using talk to come to a better understanding of a text, themselves, and each other. Both authors have had success (and many failures) in their own classrooms getting students to do so, as well as some success teaching others to foster talk in their classrooms. However, we have struggled to understand why some teachers are less able than others to foster this kind of talk consistently, even after they have demonstrated some mastery of the basic skills. To return to the fishing metaphor, we used to wonder what separates master fishermen from those who can bait and cast wherever they want—yet catch no fish.

We eventually came to the conclusion that identification of issues and decision making were at the heart of successful seminar facilitation. However, we were not sure what those issues or decisions were. We have attempted to be more explicit about a process that is often implicit and even intuitive for some teachers and a total mystery to other teachers. This book describes what we have learned about making that process explicit and using it to help all teachers become skillful facilitators.

Whatever your experience level with facilitating discussions, we hope that we begin to answer that question of "But how do you do that?" in a way that helps you combine the art, science, and magic of discussion in your own classrooms and schools. After reading this book, you should have a better understanding of the entire process of a student-centered, text-based discussion, including the basic skills, as well as what you need to balance as a facilitator and how to achieve that balance. Finally, we hope that you may be able to apply this decision-making framework to other aspects of your teaching in support of students' learning. With those goals in mind, let us begin our journey together.

ACKNOWLEDGMENTS

We owe much of our learning about leading student-centered discussions to the National Paideia Center and to the thoughtful educators who guide the center's work, including Terry Roberts, Laura Billings, Cheryl Treadway, and Robin Tilley. In addition, we are indebted to our colleagues on the National Paideia Faculty for sharing their ideas, commitment, and skill as facilitators of both students' and teachers' learning. These colleagues are too numerous to name here, but we would like to extend a special thank you to Amy Bender for her detailed feedback on an early draft of this book and to Alice Hart for her feedback on our ideas as a veteran facilitator and principal.

The rest of our learning about student-centered discussions we owe to the teachers and students with whom we have worked. In particular, we thank some of the best seminar facilitators we know: Hunter Credle, Tom Higginbotham, Shoshana Rosenbaum, and Susan Snyder, with whom we have also had the pleasure of participating in many a faculty seminar. We also owe special thanks to the teachers and students across the country who have taught us much about what it means to facilitate and participate in rich, respectful, text-based discussions, and why it is worth doing.

In particular, we thank the teachers and students of Kestrel Heights School in Durham, North Carolina: Their ideas, words, and personalities live in the vignettes and in the spirit of this book.

Turning our ideas into a book has been a longer and more challenging road than we expected, made possible by the support of many people. We thank Alan Tom for listening to our ideas and suggesting Corwin as a publisher, Tracy Smith for her supportive friendship and critical reading of an early draft of the book, and Eileen Landay for early conversations about classroom talk. We also thank Faye Zucker and Gem Rabanera at Corwin Press for their ongoing encouragement, patience, and guidance.

Finally, we thank our families for their love and support and for putting up with us during the many hours we disappeared to write.

Corwin Press gratefully acknowledges the contributions of the following reviewers:

Sylvia Jackson
Principal
Adolfo Camarillo High School
Camarillo, CA

Eric Kincaid
Science Teacher
Morgantown High School
Morgantown, WV

Douglas Llewellyn
Professor
St. John Fisher College
Rochester, NY

Cynthia Passmore
Assistant Professor
Science Education
School of Education
University of California, Davis

Kimberly C. Smith
Advanced Math Teacher/Math Department Chair
Welborn Middle School
High Point, NC

About the Authors

Michael S. Hale has served as a teacher, principal, professional developer, professor, university administrator, and educational software executive. His passion for student inquiry has resulted in many years of experience with participant-centered discussions in a wide variety of settings. A National Paideia Faculty member, he has worked with many teachers and students to develop the knowledge and skills to engage in idea- and text-based conversations. He currently spends most of his days as vice president for curriculum consulting with VitalSource Technologies in Raleigh, North Carolina, where he works with educators to transform didactic materials into more interactive digital formats. His formal education includes a BA in philosophy from Auburn University and an MA and PhD in curriculum and instruction from the University of North Carolina.

Elizabeth A. City has served as a teacher, principal, and instructional coach, primarily in North Carolina and Massachusetts. In addition to enjoying countless student-centered discussions in her own classroom, as a National Paideia Faculty member, she has worked with teachers and students across the country as they have learned to facilitate and participate in text-based conversations. Much of Liz's current work centers on supporting principals and teachers in creating collaborative communities where rich dialogue and learning for both adults and children are the norm. She is a member of the senior faculty of Boston's School Leadership Institute, where she teaches courses in using data, learning and teaching, and professional development to Boston Public School Principal Fellows. She is currently working on her doctorate at the Harvard Graduate School of Education.

PART I

Getting Started: The Science of Leading Discussions

This section is designed for teachers new to this type of classroom discussion, or for teachers who have been leading discussions by intuition. Chapter 1 focuses on the science of leading a discussion: What are the basic elements of student-centered, text-based discussions, and how do you plan for such discussions?

The Fundamentals of Facilitating

1

Student-centered discussions are conversations in which students wrestle with ideas and engage open-ended questions together through dialogue. The teacher acts as a facilitator, or guide, for the conversation, and students talk with each other rather than respond to the teacher. In this book, we focus on text-based discussions, where the conversation is grounded in some kind of rich text, which could be anything from a poem to a painting to a math problem. This chapter describes the fundamental components of student-centered, text-based discussions, and it is divided into four sections:

1. Why have student-centered discussions?

2. Essential ingredients of a discussion

3. The architecture of a discussion

4. Frequently asked questions and tips for beginners

This chapter is designed for readers who are relatively new to leading student-centered discussions and for readers who have led such discussions by instinct but have not really thought about how they do so.

WHY HAVE STUDENT-CENTERED DISCUSSIONS?

Broadly speaking, student-centered discussions help students develop intellectually and socially.[1] Through close examination and discussion of texts, students develop the skills and habits of reading analytically, listening carefully, citing evidence, disagreeing respectfully, and being open-minded. These skills are reflected in state and local standards related to oral language, discussion, reasoning, critical thinking, and reading. Increasingly, these skills are in demand both in the workforce and on state tests, which often include open-response questions. Ultimately, these skills are also demanded by our democracy, which relies on civil discourse and thoughtful exchange of ideas. In student-centered discussions, students will say things neither you nor anyone else in the room has thought about before, and students who struggle in written tasks may shine brilliantly in conversation. When all goes well, these discussions are fun in the energizing, mind-bending way of the best learning experiences.

The roots of this type of inquiry lie with the first human to ask an open-ended question about some abstraction. For example: "Hey Og, why do you think it is dark sometimes and light sometimes?" In recorded history, the basis for student-centered discussion lies in Plato's dialogues, each of which recounts a conversation about an idea or set of ideas. In most of these dialogues, the person of Socrates drives the conversation by asking questions of others. The key element of this type of inquiry is that the questioner does not give birth to the idea; rather, he or she helps others form these ideas. For this reason, Mortimer Adler (1982) contended that facilitation of discussions is akin to midwifery, helping others give birth.

The student-centered dialogue we focus on in this book is not typical in most classrooms. In most classrooms, discussion is teacher centered. In teacher-centered discussions, the teacher controls the content in an effort to cover the curriculum, or for the purposes of teaching (Barnes, 1969). Research over the last 30 years has consistently reported that the forms of teacher-centered classroom discussion are either: cases in which the teacher initiates the discussion, students respond, and the teacher then evaluates; or cases in which the teacher initiates, students respond, and then teacher gives feedback (Cazden, 1988; Sinclair & Coulthard, 1975). In both of these instances, students are mere respondents. There are certainly good pedagogical reasons for a teacher to have teacher-centered discussions in the classroom—for example, to address narrow and specific content goals or to check for understanding of previously covered content. However, when the goals for a discussion are (1) for students to deepen their understanding of ideas in a text, as well as their own ideas and the ideas of others, and (2) to develop students' ability to engage in a civil, intellectually challenging discussion of ideas, then a student-centered discussion is a more effective means to do so.

ESSENTIAL INGREDIENTS OF A STUDENT-CENTERED, TEXT-BASED DISCUSSION, AKA *SEMINAR*

Student-centered, text-based discussions are often called *seminars* or *Socratic seminars*.[2] Because our own experience draws heavily on the National Paideia Center's work with *seminars,* and because "student-centered, text-based discussion" is quite cumbersome to repeat throughout this book, we will use the term *seminar* to represent a student-centered, text-based discussion. We intentionally avoid more ambiguous language, for example, *discussion,* which could refer to teacher-centered or student-centered talk and might or might not include a text.

There are four essential ingredients to a seminar:

1. Text
2. Questions
3. Participants
4. Facilitator

Text

The first critical element of a seminar is the text. Although many valuable kinds of conversations don't revolve around a text, we focus here on conversations that do. Using a text anchors the discussion, improves students' reading and interpreting skills, and gives students the opportunity to engage deeply with important texts across disciplines. Our students often asked us whether we could have a seminar on an issue that mattered deeply to them—prejudice, justice, uniforms—to which we replied, "Sure, if you can find a text about it. Otherwise, we can discuss it in another way."

The basic definition of a high-quality text is that it is rich, it is primary, and it addresses ideas worthy of discussion. Seminar texts can be drawn from a variety of print and nonprint genres, including poems, historical documents, short stories, essays, paintings, maps, and music.

The National Paideia Center (2002) defines the characteristics of a seminar text as including:

- a collection of ideas and values
- an appropriate level of challenge and complexity for the intended participants
- relevance to both the participants and to the curricular objectives
- an appropriate degree of ambiguity.

Seminar Text Rubric			
Criteria	*3*	*2*	*1*
Ideas and Values	Addresses multiple ideas and values	Addresses some ideas and values	Addresses an idea or value
Degree of Challenge	Few participants comprehend without assistance	Some participants comprehend without assistance	All participants comprehend without assistance
Curricular Relevance	Clearly related to the curriculum	Somewhat related to the curriculum	Limited in relation to the curriculum
Ambiguity	Is open to a wide variety of interpretations	Is open to some variety of interpretations	Is open to few interpretations

Source: © National Paideia Center. Reprinted with permission.

The Paideia Seminar Text Rubric (National Paideia Center, 2002) is a useful tool for assessing whether a potential text is a good candidate for a seminar.

If a text scores mostly 3's with an occasional 2, you can consider it a good possibility. A 1 in any category is a warning sign, and a 1 in ambiguity is likely a fatal flaw because it means there is probably little to discuss. A 1 in curricular relevance, on the other hand, although less than ideal, is less crucial because even if the text is detached from what students are studying, they may be able to dig into it if the text is ambiguous, challenging, and full of ideas and values. Similarly, a 1 in degree of challenge can be OK, particularly when students are first learning how to do seminars, but seminars also offer the opportunity to tackle more difficult texts together than students might try on their own.

The first seminar Liz participated in was about the Pledge of Allegiance, a text both she and Mike have since used many times. On the Seminar Text Rubric, we would score the Pledge of Allegiance:

- 3 in Ideas and Values (liberty, justice, nation, government, allegiance, etc.)
- 1 or 2 in Degree of Challenge, depending on the participants (many students do not understand all the words in the Pledge)
- Anywhere from a 1 to 3 in Curricular Relevance, depending on the context in which it is used, but very often a 3 if used in conjunction with study of citizenship and government or as a reflection on something said daily in many schools
- 3 in Ambiguity because there are several potential interpretations of many of the words in the Pledge

We have seen teachers attempt to use excerpts from textbooks, as well as newspaper and magazine articles as texts; none of these works well in a seminar because they are not ambiguous enough. They may all be very useful texts for students to read, but they do not provide fertile ground for open-ended dialogue in a seminar context. We find it useful to think of seminar texts as classic texts. By *classic,* we mean that the texts are the sort that have endured, or will endure, because they're about the things that humans struggle with across time and cultures, like good and evil, life and death, war and peace, love, faith, betrayal, equality, honor, nature, power, and tragedy.

Finding an appropriate text is often one of the most difficult challenges for inexperienced seminar leaders. You will discover, however, that once you start looking, you will see potential texts in many places. Two resources for high-quality texts that we have found particularly helpful are:

1. The National Paideia Center (www.paideia.org), which includes sample seminar plans and the Jack and Mary McCall Library, a digital collection of texts organized by ideas, subject, and type.

2. The Touchstones Discussions Project (www.touchstones.org), which offers collections of texts for a variety of grade levels and content areas.

Questions

The next critical component of a seminar is questions. Once you have selected a text, you prepare questions to facilitate a discussion of the ideas in the text. Although you will invariably think of new questions as you listen to participants, and you will probably not ask all the questions on your list, it's important to plan for a seminar to help participants gain a deeper understanding of the text.

The most important criterion for questions is that they be open-ended. In other words, the questions should have more than one possible answer. A seminar is not the time to check for basic comprehension about what happened in the text or to make sure that students are clear on essential facts—you will do that before the seminar, as we will describe in the Architecture of a Seminar section of this chapter. Sometimes, questions might sound to students like there's one answer—for example "What's the difference between *liberty* and *freedom*?" (a question you might ask about the Pledge of Allegiance), but what you want to know is students' interpretation. In that case, you can signal that you're asking a more open-ended question by saying something like "What do *you think* the difference is between *liberty* and *freedom*?"

Questions should also be thought-provoking, meaning that students can't necessarily answer quickly and might need to return to the text and think further before responding. Finally, questions should be clear, which means that students should understand what you're asking. Often, you won't know how clear a question is until you ask it in the seminar and see the looks of understanding or puzzlement on students' faces, but a good rule of thumb is that questions should be stated as simply and succinctly as possible.

Participants

Another essential ingredient to a seminar, of course, is the participants. Seminars are appropriate for people of all ages, from kindergartners to adults. The texts, questions, and conversations will be different for different age groups and content areas, but everyone can be a participant. Although seminars develop and demand higher-order thinking skills, they are not for advanced students only. In fact, teachers are often surprised to see that their best seminar participants may be not the advanced students (some of whom are less willing to take an intellectual risk in front of their peers) but the students who might struggle with other parts of the curriculum due to their reading level or learning disability or English language proficiency. Often, these students are creative thinkers who thrive in a seminar environment where oral communication and ideas are valued.

Participants have three main tasks in any seminar:

1. Prepare

2. Participate
   Listen, think, speak, refer to text

3. Respect

Before a seminar, students should have done whatever task you've requested of them (read the text, annotate it, define unknown words, etc.), and they should have the text with them. During the seminar, students should participate, which they can do by listening to the conversation, thinking, offering comments and questions, and referring to the text. Students should also respect their classmates and the text, which they can demonstrate by using each others' names, building on others' comments, and critiquing ideas rather than people. Many teachers who do seminars regularly keep some version of the above guidelines for participation posted in their classroom.

Note about other participants: Seminars are not just for students! Seminars with faculty members and with families can be wonderful ways to discuss important ideas, rejuvenate intellectual energy, and come together as a community. In the first community seminar that we held at our school in North Carolina, parents, grandparents, students, and faculty broke into groups to have seminars on the same text, a selection from Booker T. Washington's *Up From Slavery.* Many of the parents and grandparents were a bit tentative and waited for the faculty facilitators to tell them how to interpret the text (as their teachers had always done), but the students plunged right in and led the way in a great conversation, much to the amazement and delight of their adult family members.

Facilitator

The final essential ingredient is you, the facilitator. Like the participants, you have several tasks in a seminar:

1. Prepare

2. Participate
   Listen, think, question

3. Maintain safe and respectful environment

You prepare for a seminar by selecting a text, writing questions, and planning what students need to do before and after a seminar to get them ready for the conversation and to follow up on the conversation (see the next section of this chapter for more on the before- and after-seminar components). During the seminar, you spend most of your time listening, thinking, and keeping track of the conversation by taking notes (also called *mapping* a seminar; see the final section of the book for a full explanation). You ask some questions, based on what you prepared and what students are discussing. You do not make statements—it's not your job to share your opinion or ideas, even though it can be tempting in some conversations. Your voice should not be the most frequently heard voice in the room, and this can take some getting used to, both for you and your students. Remember, you're trying to help students birth their ideas and dig deeply into the text.

Your most important task is to maintain a safe and respectful environment. The seminar must be a place where students can risk their ideas without fear of being laughed at, where all ideas are listened to, and where people are not interrupted or ignored. Remember that part of the goal of a seminar is to help students develop social skills, which, like all skills, need practice and frequent reminders as they develop. If you do not maintain a respectful environment, you will likely not have rich seminars because students either won't talk or won't share anything very interesting. The next chapter and the final chapter of this book address this topic of safety in more detail, including strategies for developing a respectful environment for a seminar.

THE ARCHITECTURE OF A SEMINAR

While a seminar may appear to the casual observer to be a free-wheeling discussion, the best seminars have a structure that supports open-ended inquiry. This structure includes pre-seminar, which prepares participants for the seminar; the seminar itself, within which there are different types of questions to guide the conversation; and post-seminar, which offers opportunities for application and extension of the ideas emerging from the seminar.

This architecture for a seminar is reflected in the Seminar Planning Form (see Resource B for a reproducible copy). The example Planning Form that follows was designed to be used with the Pledge of Allegiance in a sixth-grade classroom.

At the foundation of this structure are assumptions central to consistent success in helping students gain a deeper understanding of the text, themselves, and each other through the seminar:

- All students can and should learn to wrestle with big ideas.
- Students are capable of creating meaningful conversations about the ideas in a text.
- Students will respect each other and participate if given appropriate coaching and time.
- Students need to grapple with challenging ideas and texts.

There is value in developing listening and speaking skills. We become more literate not only by reading a book or using a pen, but also by talking to each other in situations where we can internalize and share what we read or write.

That said, the structure of the seminar is robust enough to provide a fertile ground for having rich conversations even if not all the assumptions are met in a classroom; however, success is less likely when the above conditions are not met.

Pre-Seminar

Pre-seminar activities connect the seminar to the other work of the class and help participants prepare for conversation through content and process

Seminar Planning Form

Text: The Pledge of Allegiance   Class: 6th Grade Social Studies

Pre-Seminar

Content—Present relevant background information. Prepare participants to discuss selected text.

> Before handing students a copy of the text, have them write down the Pledge from memory. Once they have done so, hand out copies of the Pledge and have students circle the words they don't know and define them. Lastly, have at least two students read the Pledge aloud.

Process—Review seminar objectives and guidelines. Prepare participants to participate in seminar discussion, and set goal[s].

> Students should look in their seminar folders to review their reflection from their last seminar and determine an individual participation goal. As a group, we will review briefly the last few seminars and develop a group goal.

Seminar Questions

Opening—Identify main ideas from the text.

> Which word do you think is most important in the Pledge of Allegiance?

Core—Focus/analyze textual details.

- Why do you think the Pledge starts with the flag and not the "republic for which it stands"?
- The Pledge was changed in 1924. It used to say "my flag" instead of "the flag." Do you think this changes the meaning? If so, how?
- What do you think the phrase "one nation under God" means? The words "under God" were added in 1954. [Read Pledge aloud without the words "under God."] Do you think the Pledge has a different meaning without those words?

Closing—Personalize and apply the textual ideas.

> What changes, if any, do you think should be made to the Pledge?

Post-Seminar

Process—Assess individual and group participation using the Fulcrum-Based Seminar Rubric (see Resource B) with students referring to recent past as well as future seminar discussion.

Content—Extend application of textual and discussion ideas; continuation of pre-seminar.

> Students have a choice of activities:

(1) Write your own pledge to something that's important to you.

(2) Write a persuasive essay about whether the Pledge should be said in school.

(3) Revise the Pledge and explain why you chose your revisions.

activities. Content activities prepare students for beginning to understand the ideas in the text. For a written text, pre-seminar content work could mean simply reading and rereading the text, or engaging in any activity that helps students master a literal interpretation of the text. In addition to comprehension, pre-seminar content work should include whatever context or background knowledge students need for the discussion. The extent of pre-seminar activities depends in part on where the seminar fits in your curriculum. If, for example, you are using a seminar to introduce a new unit and to generate questions for further study, you might do minimal pre-seminar activity beyond reading the text. If, however, the seminar is a culmination of a unit of study, the whole unit may serve as pre-seminar content development. Similarly, the extent of comprehension work you do with a text depends on both the text and the skill levels of your students. Texts like the Pledge of Allegiance or Escher prints might require minimal preparation, whereas the Gettysburg Address, a Shakespearean text, or an excerpt from Rachel Carson's *Silent Spring* might require more time and support to establish basic comprehension. Without adequate preparation, the most a seminar can be is a very good bull session.

Pre-seminar process activities help students and the facilitator prepare for having a student-centered discussion. While pre-seminar *content* activities can vary in length and depth, pre-seminar *process* activities are quick and happen right before you begin the seminar. The pre-seminar process includes a review of the roles of participants and the facilitator (see above).

During the pre-seminar process, students also set specific process goals. These goals may be for the group—for example, "We need to work on building on the ideas of others"—or individual, for example, "I need to ask more questions." Participating in a seminar is a process with which many students are not familiar, and the social component of a seminar is critical to success, both as an objective in itself and as support for the intellectual component of the seminar. As a result, working on process skills should be an explicit part of a seminar. See the strategy of Reflection in Chapter 7 and the strategy of Pre-Seminar in the Challenge Issues: Rosetta Stone section of Chapter 8 for more details on pre-seminar content and process activities.

Seminar

The seminar itself consists of three phases: opening, core, and closing; each uses a slightly different type of open-ended question. The opening question is designed to help participants identify main ideas from the text. Generally, the opening question sends participants to the text for an answer, and it is a question that all participants can answer. For example, an opening question for a seminar on the Pledge of Allegiance might be, "Which word do you think is most important in the Pledge of Allegiance?" Examples for other texts include, "What do you think a good title for this text would be?" or "Which line is most striking to you in this text?" The opening question is broad, with multiple possible answers, and provides an entry point into the text and the conversation for participants. Many facilitators do the opening question round-robin style, where every student provides an answer to the question before the facilitator opens it up for students to explain why they chose a particular answer. The round-robin is a helpful strategy for beginners but is less necessary once participants are more accustomed to the seminar process.

Core questions occur during the bulk of the conversation. They focus on particular aspects of the text and are designed to help participants dig deeply into the text. Sample core questions for the Pledge of Allegiance include, "Why do you think the Pledge starts with the flag and not the 'republic for which it stands?'" We usually plan at least three to five core questions in advance, knowing that the ones we ask will depend on what students are discussing and that we will probably think of at least one or two new questions during the seminar based on the conversation. During a seminar, you also ask follow-up questions as part of the core to probe for deeper understanding and to keep students focused on the text. Follow-up questions include: "What do you mean by _____?" "How does that statement connect to the text?" "Where else in the text do you see something that speaks to that?" "Do you agree with _____?"

The closing question helps students apply the text to their own lives. Although students may be tempted to come out of the text and make these connections earlier in the seminar, the core questions try to keep the conversation focused on the text. The closing question is the opportunity for students to personalize the text. A closing question for the Pledge of Allegiance might be: "What changes, if any, do you think should be made to the Pledge?" We plan a closing question in advance of the seminar, but sometimes, we change the question based on the conversation. Like the opening question, the closing question is broad and has many possible answers—at least as many answers as students. This format of broad-narrow-broad questions is reflected in Figure 1.1.

Post-Seminar

Following a seminar, the learning that has taken place during the seminar should be extended through various activities. As with pre-seminar activities, post-seminar activities include both process and content. To address process, directly after the seminar, the facilitator asks students to

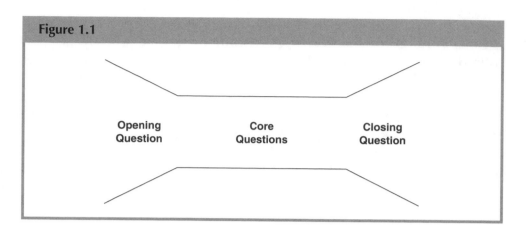

Figure 1.1

Opening Question   Core Questions   Closing Question

Used with permission of the National Paideia Center (www.paideia.org).

revisit the individual goal each of them set at the beginning of the seminar and reflect on how they did in meeting that goal. Then, the facilitator leads a group debriefing of the seminar, asking students to reflect on what the group did well and what the group could work on in their next seminar. This attention to the social component of the seminar process is critical to students' ongoing improvement of their seminar skills, which in turn enables them to participate better socially and intellectually in future seminars. It can be tempting to skip this part and leave a few more minutes for seminar discussion, but we find that the trade-off is rarely worth it.

To address content, the facilitator provides students with follow-up activities that help them extend and bring what they learned from the seminar back to their other learning. Often, post-seminar activities include writing assignments that follow directly from the seminar; other possibilities include creating artwork or role-plays based on students' interpretation and application of the ideas from the seminar. Post-seminar activity offers a good opportunity for both the facilitator and students to assess the students' thinking from a seminar. A post-seminar content activity for the Pledge of Allegiance might ask students to do one of the following: (1) write their own pledge to something that's important to them, (2) write a persuasive essay about whether the words "under God" should be included in the Pledge today (perhaps after giving students the historical context in which those words were added) or (3) revise the Pledge and explain why they chose their revisions.

A complete seminar plan includes pre-seminar, seminar, and post-seminar, as seen in the sample plan above. Additional sample plans are available at the National Paideia Center Website (www.paideia.org) and in the Center's *Seminar Sampler,* which also includes several examples of pre-seminar and post-seminar activities.

Basic Seminar Checklist

- The text chosen is appropriate for a seminar (see Seminar Text Rubric) and the development of the students.
- Prepared questions are open-ended (not leading) and designed to elicit higher-order thinking about the ideas in the text.
- The seminar plan includes pre- and post-seminar activities (see Seminar Planning Form).
- Students have all read the text and established a basic comprehension.
- The room is set up to allow all participants to make eye contact with each other (e.g., circle or square).

This checklist can be used to ensure that the fundamental aspects of the seminar have been addressed prior to beginning the discussion.

FREQUENTLY ASKED QUESTIONS AND TIPS FOR BEGINNERS

Frequently Asked Questions

What does a seminar look like? Participants sit so they can all make eye contact with each other, in a circle or square, depending on what's possible in the room. The facilitator is part of the circle. There is no hand raising or being called on. Participants have a copy of the text in front of them. Most of the talk comes from participants, with the facilitator asking questions occasionally. Sometimes, there is silence as participants and the facilitator think.

How long does a seminar take? The length of a seminar will vary somewhat based on the age of students (shorter seminars for younger students) and the text, but a rule of thumb is about 45 minutes to an hour for the discussion. The length of pre-seminar and post-seminar activities will depend on what's appropriate for the text you've chosen, your students, and your curriculum. Some pre-seminar and post-seminar activities may be short enough to occur within the same class period as the discussion, some may be done as homework before and after the seminar, and others may require lengthier, in-class time.

For what subjects and grade levels is the seminar format appropriate? As we noted earlier in this chapter, a seminar is appropriate for all grade levels. Seminars for elementary students tend to be 20 to 45 minutes in length and spend more time focused on the social elements of the seminar process, particularly in the early grades. Seminars can be done in all subjects, including English/language arts, math, social studies, science, foreign language, art, music, and physical education. Sometimes, seminars happen outside of content areas, where everyone in a team, grade level, or sometimes the whole school engages in seminars about the same text. Schoolwide seminars can be particularly powerful for generating a conversation about common texts and ideas.

How many people can participate in the same seminar? The short answer is that you can make a seminar work for almost any size class or group that you have. The longer answer is that you want enough people to have a range of ideas for the conversation, but not so many people that participants can't find enough space in the conversation to contribute their ideas. In our experience, the balance of those two considerations usually falls between 15 and 35 participants, but good seminars are possible outside of that range. If you have more than 35 participants, you might try having some participants outside the seminar circle as process observers (see Fishbowl strategy in Chapter 7 of this book for an example of this). We've also seen teachers with very large classes have a seminar with half the class while the other half of the class works independently. If you have the luxury of space and another facilitator, you might also split the group into two groups and have separate seminars using the same text.

How often should I do a seminar? You need to do a seminar often enough for both you and students to practice. As with any other set of skills or classroom activity, especially when you are all first learning it, it's important to practice frequently so that everyone learns the routine and how to do it well. Initially, that frequency can translate into weekly seminars. Beyond that, the answer to this question depends on your goals and your curriculum. Some teachers we know do weekly seminars; others do them biweekly, once a month, or even once a quarter. We tend to see seminars more frequently in social studies and English language-arts classes, in part because it's easier to find high-quality texts for those subjects, but we know plenty of math and science teachers who use seminars regularly in their classrooms. A companion question that we often hear is "How do I fit seminars into all the other things I've got to do?" The underlying concern here is that seminars take too much time away from an otherwise jammed list of things to cover. The important thing to consider is that seminar isn't an add-on to those other things—it should be part of the curriculum and should be helping you reach your objectives.

A seminar is so open ended. Is any answer "right"? Although a seminar is open ended, that doesn't mean anything people say in a seminar is "right." Sometimes, students will say things that are factually incorrect, like "Well, back in the day when Thomas Jefferson wrote the Pledge of Allegiance, it was OK to use the phrase 'under God,' so I think we have to look at it from that historical perspective." Often, another student will correct that kind of wrong answer, but if the answer goes uncorrected, it's up to you to decide whether correcting it during the seminar is important for students' understanding of the text. In this case, you would probably clarify that Thomas

Jefferson didn't write the Pledge, ask if anyone knows when it was written, and then ask a question about how that historical perspective affects the way students think about the Pledge. If the error is less critical to the conversation, you might not interrupt the seminar to correct but wait until after the seminar to clarify it. The other kind of "not right" answer is the kind that is unsupported by the text. This is not very likely to happen with the Pledge of Allegiance, but it crops up in discussions of other texts, where a student might say something like, "That character is crazy" or "The author doesn't like poor people," either of which could be a defensible inference to draw from a text but could also be a statement that a student can't find support for in the text at all. If it looks to you like students are giving this sort of a response, simply ask them what in the text supports their statement.

Tips for Beginners

If you are new to seminar facilitation, or if your students are new to the process, here are a few things to keep in mind:

Start small. In the beginning, keep seminars short in length (10 minutes for young students; 20 minutes for older students)—better for the seminar to end with students wanting to talk more than to end in prolonged silence. Also, use seminar texts that are short and not too demanding in terms of reading comprehension (e.g., the Pledge of Allegiance). You don't want to overwhelm students in the beginning. Build up to longer seminars and more challenging texts.

Focus on the social parts of the seminar first. Yes, we know you want to have sophisticated conversations about difficult texts with your students. However, most students aren't used to being asked for their opinion without ongoing feedback and commentary from a teacher, and they're not necessarily used to having intellectual conversations with their peers. They have to learn how to do those things. It's OK if the first few seminars are not the most intellectual conversations, focusing more on students learning how to do a seminar, how not to interrupt each other, how to refer to a text, how to disagree, and so on. The intellectual parts will come, once you have established the social parts of a seminar.

Use different kinds of text. Use a variety of texts, including both print and nonprint texts. You'll find that individual students respond differently to texts.

Plan with someone else. Writing good questions and thinking of good pre- and post-seminar activities is almost always easier with someone else, so see if you can enlist a colleague to plan with you.

Be careful about how many seminars you do in a day. If you see multiple groups of students in a day, you might be tempted to do a seminar with each group on the same day. Be warned that seminars are exhausting—even though you don't talk much as a facilitator, you're concentrating so hard during the seminar that the process is surprisingly tiring. We occasionally have done five seminars in a day, but we could barely talk or think at the end (much less be great facilitators for that fifth seminar).

Don't get discouraged. Sometimes, seminars flop (even for us, and we've done zillions of them). And sometimes, it can take a long time for students to develop the social and intellectual skills needed for successful seminars—all the more reason to keep trying seminars because students clearly need work in that area. Trust that the process will work for you and your students. The rest of this book is designed to help you think about what's happening in a seminar and how to respond as a facilitator. You will eventually have seminars that soar and reaffirm why you are a teacher.

The fundamental skills outlined in this chapter—selecting texts, asking questions, and designing pre- and post-seminar activities—form the blueprint for a successful seminar. They are, in a sense, the science of creating a collaborative, intellectual dialogue in the classroom. However, as anyone who has tried such dialogue can attest, mastering these skills does not guarantee a successful seminar. To probe more deeply into the art and magic of seminar facilitation, we turn our attention to the multiple decisions a facilitator makes during a seminar.

Note to beginners: You may want to have a few seminars before reading the next chapter.

REFERENCES

Adler, M. (1982). *The Paideia proposal.* New York: Macmillan.

Barnes, D. (1969). *Language, the learner, and school.* Baltimore, Maryland: Penguin.

Cazden, C. (1988). *Classroom discourse.* Portsmouth, NH: Heinemann.

National Paideia Center. (2002) *Teaching for understanding: Seminar instruction.* Chapel Hill, NC: Author.

Sinclair J., & Coulthard, R. M. (1975). *Towards an analysis of discourse: The English used by teachers and pupils.* Oxford: Oxford University Press.

NOTES

1. We are deeply indebted to the National Paideia Center, with whom we have learned much about facilitating student-centered, text-based discussions, which the National Paideia Center refers to as *seminars*. We draw on the center's work heavily throughout this chapter. Readers interested in more detail than we provide here will find useful resources on the center's Website, www.paideia.org

2. A simple Google search of *Socratic seminar* yields more than 20,000 hits.

PART II

Becoming
a Skillful
Facilitator

*The Art and Magic of Leading
Student-Centered Discussions*

Once you know the science of facilitating seminar, it's time to delve into the art and magic of the process. Do you wonder why some discussions soar and others limp? Are you unsure what to do when your seminar isn't going according to plan? Do you notice that your colleague down the hall seems to be a natural facilitator and wonder why it looks so easy for her? As a facilitator, you make dozens of decisions during a seminar, many of which you may not even be aware of. Such decisions include: Should I ask a question now, or let the conversation go on a little longer?

This section expands on our earlier work. Michael S. Hale and Elizabeth A. City. "'But How Do You *Do* That?': Decision Making for the Seminar Facilitator" in *Inquiry and the Literary Text: Constructing Discussions in the English Classroom.* Ed. James Holden and John S. Schmit. Urbana, Illinois: National Council of Teachers of English, 2002.

If now, what question should I ask? Do I need to worry that these six students haven't said anything yet? Was that comment disrespectful enough for me to interrupt seminar, or should I let it go and handle it later? Are students too far off the text, or is this conversation relevant?

The decisions you make help determine whether your seminar succeeds or fails. Thus, instead of just acting on instinct, it's important to have a way of thinking about those decisions. You know how to choose a text, write questions, and design pre-seminar and post-seminar activities, and yet, you don't have perfect seminars every time. Don't worry—neither do we. But we know how to think about what's happening during seminar and what kinds of decisions we're making, which helps us have good seminars more often. This section offers a framework for understanding the decision-making process of effective facilitation.

The framework consists of four dimensions of a seminar: *safety, authentic participation, challenge,* and *ownership*. We call these four dimensions *fulcrums* because they are the leverage points on which seminars should be balanced; you can use them to guide your decisions. To help students develop a deeper understanding of the text, the facilitator is constantly assessing the conversation by asking, "What, if anything, is preventing students from developing a deeper understanding of the text, themselves, and others?" The fulcrums provide categories into which most answers to this question fit. In this section, we describe the fulcrums and a decision-making model for applying them.

Each of the next four chapters is devoted to one of the four fulcrums: safety, authentic participation, challenge, and ownership. Each fulcrum chapter begins and ends with a vignette from a seminar we have either facilitated or observed. The opening vignette illustrates a discussion in which a particular fulcrum is out of balance, and the closing vignette shows one in which it is in balance. The body of each chapter describes the fulcrum and includes examples of how it can be identified and corrected. In the final chapter of this section, we describe a decision-making model that includes all four fulcrums and provide an explanation of each step.

2 Safety

Many students are participating, and there are no side conversations, sarcasm, or teasing.

Attacking Personalities		Tiptoeing

Indicators:

- Hurt students
- Nonparticipation
- Future reluctance to participate

Safety

Indicators:

- Few ideas challenged
- Intellectually weak seminar
- Stale environment

The last seminar in Mr. Monroe's ninth-grade biology class didn't go well. Students had dutifully offered a few ideas, but the conversation had long silences, and everyone seemed a bit bored. But today was different. Today, students were on the edge of their seats, leaning forward, watching each speaker with all the attention they might give a boxing match. They were looking closely at their text, following each speaker's point, looking to see where they could add to someone's point or disagree based on the text. And the conversation! "I can't believe these are ninth graders," Mr. Monroe thought. A bit smugly, he congratulated himself that he had made it possible for these students to comment so brilliantly on a section of Darwin's *Origin of Species*. And he even had a witness. The principal had chosen this day to sit in and observe the seminar. As he mentally patted himself on the back, he returned his focus to the conversation.

"The 'survival of the fittest' is indisputable," said Seth. "It's all around us. Every animal we see is evidence." "OK," said Timothy. "But I don't think 'survival of the fittest' explains who I am. It's just a theory." Timothy's comment was met with many headshakes and scattered applause from a few of his classmates. "Timothy, I disagree with you," said Francine, rather emphatically. She held up pictures of some of Darwin's finches from the Galapagos. "They are different, just like we are all different." As she continued to make her point, several students looked like they might explode with their ideas before they could share them. Sandy's comment—"Yeah, it's like that thing Mr. Shellman told us about geologic time. We have a hard time understanding how long it takes for animals to change and how little time humans have been on the Earth"—was completely lost in the storm of shouts and applause that erupted as Timothy and Francine and their supporting casts continued to make their points. The conversation was flying back and forth, around the circle. Students were talking passionately about their ideas.

But Sandy had his head in his hands, frustrated that no one heard his point. Francine was either going to cry or yell louder. Timothy had resorted to "That's just stupid" to back up his ideas. Matthew slumped in his chair and shot the ceiling a bored "I-get-enough-of-this-yelling-at-home" look. Denaya looked like she had a carefully thought-out point to contribute if she could just jump in. Class ended, and the students left the room still arguing about natural selection and evolution. Mr. Monroe checked in with the principal later, expecting to hear something about how interesting the conversation was and how impressed she was with the depth of students' thinking. Instead she said, "It was a little too Jerry Springer, wasn't it?"

Because it lacked an intellectually and emotionally safe environment, the seminar recounted above wasn't wildly successful—instead, it was just wild. During a safe seminar, Sandy's comment would have been heard, and neither he nor Matthew would have disengaged. Creating and maintaining a safe environment is the first condition necessary for successful seminars. Safety refers to the emotional and psychological safety of the students. Although you may have some students willing to share ideas without regard to the format or climate created, most students, particularly at the secondary level, are not comfortable enough with themselves intellectually to offer ideas about which they are unsure. Given that engaging in a discussion of ideas requires some intellectual risk, students must feel that their vulnerability will be protected. In addition, the relative safety of a seminar setting can impact the success of both present and future seminars. It will take a while for the above-mentioned class to believe that the seminar is a safe space to share ideas. Until then, only the most verbal, confident, or combative students will participate. The emotional and intellectual safety of students must be established if all students are expected to engage in student- and idea-centered discussions.

RECOGNIZING SAFETY ISSUES

Had Mr. Monroe asked, "What, if anything, is preventing the students from coming to a better understanding of the text, themselves, and others?" he would have noted a number of issues, including student indignation, student frustration, and disrespectful comments. Once he noticed one of these issues, he might have recognized that safety was slipping away. To balance this fulcrum, a facilitator must keep the following questions in mind:

- What is the tone of the conversation?
- What is the atmosphere of the setting?

Tone of the Discussion

The tone of the conversation affects its content. Although Timothy and Francine were both engaging directly with the text and finding support for their positions, their exchange had become a debate, complete with a cheering audience, à la Jerry Springer. This created a setting in which the primary participants could only dig into their foxholes a little deeper, while the students who were paying attention were thinking about the argument rather than about the ideas in the text. Timothy and Francine were still finding support for their positions; however, the tone of their conversation excluded other viewpoints and caused both of them to listen for flaws in the argument of the other, rather than genuinely considering the "other side." The tone also prevented Sandy's comment from bringing thoughtful consideration back into the conversation; instead, his remark was lost in the noise.

The tone of the seminar needs to be one of respect for all of the students participating, as well as the text. The students do not need to agree with one another, but they have to respect differences of ideas. In fact, a successful seminar is built on the understanding that emerges from different ideas. Without this respect, a conversation can evolve into a talk show free-for-all, marked by righteous indignation.

For students, two of the primary goals of a seminar are to learn how to understand others and to develop a willingness to have their ideas challenged. The key is helping students disagree agreeably. Most students need to be taught these skills, as they often assume that any challenge is a personal attack and respond defensively. The first step is defining the difference between challenging a personality and challenging a person's idea. At the core of this skill is treating everyone and every idea with respect, a worthy approach in any setting. However, respecting all ideas doesn't mean that all ideas are equal and well-supported. Helping students to understand this distinction is critical and difficult and will be discussed further in the sections on the authentic participation and challenge fulcrums.

Atmosphere of Safety and Respect

To create and maintain an atmosphere of emotional safety and respect, you as a facilitator must be aware of how both you and your students act and react during the seminar. You must do this prior to and during the seminar. Setting goals prior to the seminar helps focus students on the seminar process and their responsibility for contributing to a safe and productive seminar. In addition, the tone for a safe environment should be set during a discussion of the guidelines for seminar participation.

To create an atmosphere conducive to sharing and challenging ideas, the facilitator should consider the overall climate of the classroom. What kind of relationship do you have with your students? Are students encouraged to ask questions? Are students used to working in groups? These are important questions to ask because the culture of a classroom can be difficult to modify for a seminar.

CREATING A CULTURE OF INQUIRY

Seminars are most successful in terms of student understanding when they are conducted in a culture of inquiry; therefore, if a culture of inquiry does not exist in the classroom, it must be created. If a culture of inquiry already exists in the classroom, then establishing an emotionally and intellectually safe environment may not be as difficult. However, this is not necessarily true. For example, one of the authors spent time in an advanced placement history classroom in which the students and teacher had created a culture of inquiry. Evidence of this culture could be found in the work they had done, including a video documentary of a local historic cemetery produced by the students themselves, as well as in a lively classroom full of questions and discussion. Unfortunately, sarcasm and competition were also a part of this culture. That is, although the students and teacher pushed each other intellectually during other classroom activities, they also traded witticisms in a friendly, yet competitive way. This type of culture in not uncommon in intellectually challenging and stimulating environments; indeed, it is often the culture of graduate school. However, sarcasm uses wit as a method to wound or ridicule, and it does not support a seminar, where ideas should be shared rather than wielded.

The Danger of Sarcasm

Seminar should be a time when sarcasm is rarely, if ever, permitted. Humor is certainly acceptable, but not at the expense of others. If laughter occurs in a seminar, it should be students laughing *with* others, not *at* one another. This can be difficult to achieve for students at the secondary level, a time when students often cover their own insecurities by assailing the vulnerability of others. Attacking *people* is never appropriate in a seminar;

challenging other people's *ideas*, however, is vital for increasing understanding. An atmosphere must develop in which all ideas can be discussed and challenged without students becoming personally offended.

If students are offended or fear that their comment will be met with sarcasm or other disrespectful behavior, they might tiptoe around ideas. In a seminar that features tiptoeing, most students are quiet; sometimes, one student dominates, and everyone else tiptoes. When students do speak, they don't challenge anyone else's ideas or offer an idea beyond a straightforward observation that would be hard for anyone else to challenge. Sometimes, they say, "I agree," without elaboration. Tiptoeing often happens when seminar participants don't know each other well, when they don't understand the seminar process yet, or when there is some kind of issue with disrespect. Students in these seminars will often say later (or sometimes during the seminar) that "this is boring." And they're right.

Feedback During a Seminar

As the facilitator, you can help by reminding students of your role during the conversation. Like the role of the participants, the role of the facilitator sounds simple, but it is not necessarily easy to implement. During the seminar, you should help the students attain a deeper understanding of the text, themselves, and each other. Facilitators neither offer ideas about the text nor give positive or negative feedback to a particular student. Indeed, you may not even look at the student who is speaking because you don't want students to be focusing on you. However, it is critical for you to inform students that you will not be giving feedback and might not look at them as they speak; otherwise, students may perceive the lack of feed back as de facto negative feedback. Most students are used to teacher feedback; if it's lacking, students might feel uncomfortable, and consequently unsafe, unless they understand the reasons behind the lack of feedback. We often remind students that it is their conversation, not ours, and that it's our job to help them have that conversation.

Facilitator feedback during the seminar should concern the degree to which students are following the guidelines of seminar behavior. When providing this type of feedback, you need to make it clear to the students that you are stepping out of your role as facilitator and back into the role of teacher. Many teachers, including the authors, use the term "time-out" to signify to students this change of roles. During the time-out, you might ask the students what they were doing well during the seminar and what they need to work on, or you might point out some examples of students politely disagreeing with other students.[1] For example, in the opening vignette, Mr. Monroe should have taken a "time-out" as soon as the tone of students became indignant, as was certainly the case by the time the clapping started. In the time-out, he could have reminded students about the importance of a respectful environment. He could have also taken the time to point out what a good job some of the participants had done in finding support for their positions. If this reminder and positive reinforcement did not work, a role-play might be used to show the way a respectful conversation takes place. Following the time-out, Mr. Monroe would call "time-in" to return to the seminar and his role as facilitator.

It is worth pointing out that the reason Mr. Monroe did not notice these things is because there were many things to be excited about, as the opening vignette demonstrates. Students were engaged and excited about words and ideas written almost 150 years ago. This is something we should celebrate. However, the conversation had a lot of unrealized potential, and the lack of safety may have impeded the development of ideas not only in this seminar, but also in future seminars.

A Climate of Respect

It is difficult to overemphasize the importance of establishing a climate of respect, which is the foundation for the balancing of safety. The seminar should be an almost sacred time. Before moving on to focus on any of the other fulcrums, the facilitator must create a climate that allows students to share ideas, to hear each other speak, and to challenge each other's ideas. There may be some students who take much longer to learn how to respect other students and the seminar process.[2] Only after creating this climate should the facilitator begin to focus on the next fulcrum, authentic participation.

"How did your first seminar with the tenth-graders go?" Mr. Monroe asked Ms. Rose during the first week of the new school year.

"It was amazing," she replied. "I couldn't believe how polite and respectful they were compared to some of the students I've had before."

"What do you think was the difference?" he inquired.

"Well, I'm not sure," Ms. Rose said, "but it might have been because we had a long discussion beforehand about what kind of atmosphere we wanted to have so that everyone could talk and share their ideas. We talked about wanting a safe classroom so that people could risk their ideas and we had a wonderfully civil conversation about Gwendolyn Brooks's 'Children of the Poor.' They really worked hard on the lines that include *hate* and *harmony*."

"Even Timothy and Francine?" Mr. Monroe asked because this was the group he had the year before.

"Especially Timothy and Francine," she replied. "I think they know how important safety is. We're off to a good start."

NOTES

1. For a more complete summary of "time-out" and other techniques for attaining and maintaining safety, please see Chapter 8.

2. One student we know spent a whole year being removed from seminars due to disrespectful behavior. The next year, however, he assumed leadership in teaching new students what kinds of behavior are and are not acceptable because, as he noted in a rather exasperated tone, "They just don't know how to do it yet."

3 Authentic Participation

Student comments refer directly to the text or to another participant's comments, and are made in a respectful manner.

Nonparticipation   **Superficial Participation**

Indicators: *Indicators:*
- Silent students   - Mere talking
- Unfocused students   - Unsupportable
- Little interaction among   statements
  participants   - Expert-parroting

**Authentic
Participation**

This was the fourth seminar for Ms. Chang's seventh-grade world history class. They were studying civil wars, so she chose a text that was rich and accessible— Pablo Picasso's "Guernica." Before she began, she asked students to share ideas with a partner about the most intriguing and important elements of the mural. There was a loud buzz of ideas. After each person shared the word they felt best described the emotion of the mural, she followed with her standard first line: "Now I'm just going to open it up for anyone who would like to explain why they chose the words they did or has something else to say about the text." And then she waited. And waited. And waited. "Shoot," she thought. "I forgot to warn them that I will outwait them during silence, so they needn't wait for me to rescue them." She started getting a little nervous as the clock ticked on.

As she waited, she thought about the seminar the day before with another class on this same text. With them, the problem was not so much silence as it was not *enough* silence. Each student had his or her own idea and waited patiently to share it. One student caught himself several times as he started to interrupt people. Eventually, he found an opening and shared his idea with pride. Unfortunately, the conversation had already taken four turns away from his idea, but he had been so eager to share his thought that he didn't listen to other people's thoughts. Back with today's group, she reassured herself that they had all had much to say to their partners not two minutes ago. Sure enough, someone finally breathed deeply and said, "Well I chose *mourning* because . . ."

This fulcrum balances mere talking, in which participants make comments without much thought, and silence. The middle ground is authentic participation, defined by thoughtful, considered statements and questions by the participants. In the seminars recounted above, Ms. Chang's current class, although silent for a while, was authentically participating; her class from the previous day, on the other hand, was not, despite much sharing of comments. The talkative group is typical of a class that has recently established a climate of safety. A class at this stage of development has often not yet learned to focus conversation but is very much ready to learn to authentically participate.

RECOGNIZING AUTHENTIC PARTICIPATION ISSUES

This fulcrum follows safety because once safety is established, it is tempting for facilitators to be so pleased that students are making statements, being polite, and referencing the text that they don't focus on the quality and depth of the participation. Some students will make statements simply to seek attention or because they know they are supposed to, not because they have genuinely reflected on the ideas in the text. However, once focused on this fulcrum, the seminar facilitator can gauge the authenticity of the seminar and help students become focused on the task of developing a deeper understanding of the text. The questions a facilitator keeps in mind to balance this fulcrum include:

- Are students participating primarily to seek attention?
- Is the conversation text-focused?
- Are students jumping from comment to comment without exploring them in depth?
- Is the talking merely a sharing of ideas, or are students responding to one another?

Attention-Seeking Participation

Most teachers can recognize when a student is participating simply to gain attention. Some attention-seeking behavior, like making noises, interrupting, and making fun of others, is eliminated by creating a safe atmosphere. Other attention-seeking behavior, however, is within the bounds of "safe" but prevents students from participating in an authentic manner. This kind of behavior includes seemingly random and unsupported statements, rambling statements that seem to be made up after the student has begun speaking, and reference to an expert outside the seminar rather than an original idea (adult participants are most susceptible to this "expert parroting"). An effective response to this type of participation is to ask the student, "Can you show us where you find support for that in the text?" Asking students to support their answers will force most students both to engage the text and to find some linkage to their comment, or simply to pull out of the conversation until they find some connection to the text.

Text-Focused Participation

Students sometimes build nicely supported arguments that are unrelated to the text. For example, during a unit exploring how to "read" different kinds of texts, one class did a seminar on a world map. At one point in the conversation, two students began discussing which country produced the best animation. The students began outlining their differing positions, using the quality of particular animated works before the facilitator asked them if they could find support for their assertions in the text, which they could not. However, the facilitator also told them that their arguments had the makings of a wonderful follow-up research topic for later debate and that she would make a note to bring it up at a later time outside of the seminar.

In this case, the students were not authentically participating because they knew that the conversation was off-topic; however, they were being respectful and supporting their ideas. As a result, it was important for the facilitator to encourage their enthusiasm but also to remind them that a seminar on a world map was not the appropriate place to have a debate about the relative merits of Japanese versus American animation.

As the map seminar became more text focused, the conversation moved to questions about the decisions made by the cartographer. One question generated by a student and explored with some focus was "Why do you think the map is not drawn so that the equator is in the middle of the map?" During the discussion of this question, most students participated authentically and only a few comments were made to draw laughter. When inauthentic individual comments are made during a focused conversation, the facilitator addresses them directly only if students are becoming distracted and the conversation is derailed. If students ignore the inauthentic comments, then you simply make a note on the seminar map (see Chapter 7) and discuss authentic participation with the individual student at a later time.

Reflective Activity

Authentic participation requires more than alternately making statements; it requires reflection. Reflective activity is arguably one of the least emphasized intellectual skills in the United States. Although it is certainly developed in many classrooms around the country, it is usually practiced through writing (essays, journal writing, reading responses, etc.). Reflective activity is rarely honored in a group setting or as an aspect of discussions. By reflective activity, we mean thoughtfulness (in the sense of full of thought) put into action through the spoken word. In a seminar, this means that students should consider both the text and what others have said before speaking.

In a good seminar, there may be periods of silence that last for up to one minute (even two on occasion). A period of silence this long, which can feel like an eternity to everyone in the room, is fine if it is used by students to think about the text. When silence fills the air during a discussion in a typical classroom, it is often quickly filled by a teacher asking another question or sharing knowledge about the topic. Although this type of classroom interaction may be appropriate for some discussions, especially those in which a teacher is leading students to a particular understanding of a topic, it allows students to be "off the hook" in terms of generating their own thoughts and ideas about the topic. Students will often shift into cognitive neutral if they know the teacher will fill the silence; however, if the teacher as facilitator is patient and waits for students to break the silence, the rewards are often a conversation of much greater depth.

You can help students endure and use silence well by warning them during pre-seminar activities why you may not speak if it gets silent. We remind students that silence can be good: It means people are thinking. We sometimes use a watch to time the silence (and discover that what felt like five minutes was only 30 seconds). Sharing with students the length of the longest wait time during the debriefing of the seminar can be valuable in preparing for future seminars and encouraging silence.

Assessing Pauses in Conversation

All pauses in the conversation, however, are not worthy of reflection time. Sometimes, the silence means students need to be asked a probing question or to move to a different idea in the text. The facilitator must consider why there is silence: Is it because the current line of thinking has been completely explored, or is it because the students are still skirting around the surface of a text waiting to be told what to think? If it is the former, then you might need to ask a question that forces students to consider a different idea in the text or to consider their current line of thinking in light of some other part of the text. For example, "Given what you are saying about the concept of reincarnation, how do you think that fits with line 18 and 19 in the poem?" If, however, the students are simply being intellectually lazy or need to go back and review more of the text, then promoting reflection by asking another question and practicing wait-time may be the best decision. However, sometimes, silence is the most effective facilitator response.

Facilitator Is Not the Focus

The final indicator of authentic participation is whether the students are talking directly to the facilitator or to each other. If they are talking to you, they may still be waiting for you to tell them the "right answer" or to give them some direction. Until they cease to look to the facilitator after every comment, the seminar will never develop into a natural conversation. To combat this common behavior, you must prepare the class prior to the seminar, telling them that you will not look at them, not because you are being rude but because you want to encourage them to talk with each other. You can further help students by not looking at the student who is talking during the seminar. This lack of eye contact can be particularly challenging for teachers. Teachers are used to giving (and students are used to getting) positive reinforcement through eye contact, head nods, and little words of encouragement. In student-centered discussions, however, the audience for comments and the source of feedback should be students, not the teacher. Otherwise, the teacher is still at the center of the conversation. Therefore, you have to train yourself not to respond to students. During the seminar, the group may need a reminder, but simply looking away to another student or down at notes is often enough to remind a student to look at other participants. Remind them that a seminar is their conversation, not yours. Once students understand how to authentically participate, it is time to begin focusing on the challenge of the seminar.

> "Well, I disagree with Jennifer," said Dominic. "If you don't *contend,* then you cannot win. Sure, 'no one can contend with you.' But, you've got to play the game."
>
> "I agree with Dominic," said Manuel. "Doesn't *contend* mean compete? We live in a competitive society."

"I've changed my mind a bit," Jennifer followed up. "I agree that we live in a competitive society. But the poet is trying to say that all are losers, who contend."

"Wait a second," Carlos interjected. "What if this is true? I mean, how will the economy grow?"

"It's a poem," replied Naila. "It's supposed to be symbolic."

Ms. Bernardi jumped in. "Does it matter that this text was written 2500 years ago in China?"

After a bit of reflection, LaDeidre said, "People in all civilizations try to explain things about their lives, but people in very different cultures still live similar human lives" . . . And the conversation about the excerpt from the *Tao Te Ching* continued.

After the seminar, Ms. Bernardi asked students what they did well during the seminar. "Well, we stayed on the text and didn't get distracted," said one student. "Yup, and we looked at each other when we talked." "And we followed up on each other's points instead of just blurting out whatever we wanted to say."

"What can we work on next time?" she asked. "Well, we got a little stuck on that whole competition thing and not everyone participated," replied another student. . . .

Challenge

Student comments address the complexities
of the ideas in the text and deepen understanding.

Popcorn		Rosetta Stone

Indicators:
- Unsupportable lines of inquiry pursued
- Supportable lines of inquiry not followed up
- Idea-hopping

Challenge

Indicators:
- Little or no participation
- "Stabs-in-the-dark"
- Circular conversation

Students in the senior humanities class were agreeing and disagreeing with one another in a respectful manner while delving into Plato's "Allegory of the Cave." However, they seemed tentative and they gave support by simply reading a quotation from the text. Rarely was an idea strengthened or deepened. Shana noted, "The shadows on the wall might represent reality as we see it; however, Plato believes truth is found outside the Cave and in the light."

After this comment, Ms. Milani expected numerous other students to jump in and further this line of thinking or offer a different interpretation, but nothing happened. She followed up with a question about truth and the shadows on the wall. This was met with silence, until, after about two minutes, William, one of the most hard-working and thoughtful students, looked up and said, "I don't have a clear picture of the Cave in my head."

Ms. Milani was almost annoyed. William was way behind in the conversation. Didn't he read the text? Then she looked around the circle quickly. Robert and Eldrick seemed about to start talking football, and most other students looked frustrated or puzzled. She asked if anybody in the group felt they had a good picture of the Cave in their head and received few affirmative responses. "Well, maybe we should all come to some agreement about the description of the cave. . . ."

I n the above conversation, the major concepts in the text—"truth" and "the good"—are certainly challenging, and some students were ready to delve into them. However, most of the students had been left at the gate because they didn't have a literal understanding of the allegorical Cave before the conversation turned to the symbolic. In this case, the facilitator seemed to understand that the issue was lack of idea development; however, she didn't know the cause. Fortunately, William came to the rescue by noting that he didn't have a picture of the Cave in his head, and the facilitator made the correct decision that challenge was the issue. So, she stopped the seminar and returned to the description of the Cave.

However, had William not been confident enough to admit that he had no idea what the Cave looked like, the seminar might have continued without him and many others who never understood the foundations to the conversation. For these participants, the text had been a Rosetta stone, and they had no one to translate the hieroglyphics. This vignette illustrates the need to monitor the relative challenge of the conversation for all participants. The two most important decisions regarding the level of intellectual challenge for students in the seminar are choice of text and questions.

RECOGNIZING CHALLENGE ISSUES

Because most classrooms and schools include students (and teachers) with a wide range of experiences and intellectual development, this can be a difficult fulcrum for the facilitator. Both the questions and the text must be challenging enough to force even the most intellectually mature students to stretch their minds, without being beyond comprehension by the least mature students. To maintain this balance, you as the facilitator must monitor the relative understanding of all students. You must be closely attuned to more than just the students who are talking; you must also focus on who is daydreaming, aching to speak, talking to a neighbor, or looking bewildered. There are a number of ways to do this, including a periodic scanning of the participants and mapping of a seminar (see Chapter 7). Questions to consider when determining whether an issue in the seminar is related to challenge include:

- Are only a few students participating?
- Are the same points being made over and over in different words?
- Do questions require the students to stop and reflect and return to the text?

At the center of all conversation in a seminar should be the ideas inherent in the text. Assuming a text has been chosen that is rich in ideas, the facilitator works to help participants focus the conversation on ideas in the text.

Assessing Understanding

In the case of the slow-moving seminar discussion during which few students are making statements or asking questions, the facilitator has to determine whether students are ready to answer a question or discuss the text. Sometimes, a question is asked at too high a level for that particular moment in the seminar, or students need to have a minimal understanding or experience with certain concepts before they can answer the question at hand. For example, in a discussion of Gwendolyn Brooks's poem "To the Diaspora," when one student asked, "Why do you think Brooks spelled *Afrika* with a *k*?," he was met with silence. The facilitator thought it was a marvelous question but observed the class's silence and realized from the many blank looks she saw that the other students weren't ready to think about it yet because it was still the first few minutes of the seminar. She guided the conversation to a different question by saying, "What an interesting question, Antonio. I'm not sure we're ready to think about that yet. Let's think about who the speaker of the poem is and who the audience for the poem might be and then we can return to the question of why *Afrika* is spelled with a *k*."

Off-Topic Conversation

Off-topic conversations are a common occurrence during weak seminars, in part because they offer students a defense against challenge or uncertainty. You as facilitator need to handle such conversations in a way that leads the conversation back to the ideas in the text. First, you must be able to recognize an off-topic conversation. In most cases, this is clear, but some off-topic conversations and comments are less obvious. For example, in a seminar on Langston Hughes's poem "Theme for English B," suppose a student mentioned that his Aunt Edith was a poet and used to write poems about her dog. To determine whether this student is going to be able to contribute to the understanding of the ideas in the text, you could simply ask the student, "Can you tell us how your Aunt Edith's dog poems relate to the ideas in the text?" The student may say "no" or he may continue his story, emphasizing how his aunt told him that she liked to use her dog poems to tell her own personal stories, just as Hughes seems to be.

In a similar apparent non sequitur, a usually quiet student inter-rupted a seminar on "The Body Rituals of the Nacirema," during which the concepts of *primitive* and *uncivilized* were being discussed: "Are you saying my parents are *primitive*?" No one was quite sure what she meant, but the facilitator asked her how her comment related to the text. The student went on to eloquently express how her parents grew up in mud huts in Africa and how they both fit and contradicted the author's and her peers' definition of *primitive.*

Repetitive Ideas and Statements

There are also times in a discussion when students are very focused on one idea. In such a case, you as the facilitator should address this question: Are students continuing to develop a deeper and more complex under-standing of the idea, or are they restating the same assertions using differ-ent words? If the conversation is continuing to develop a more complex understanding of an idea, then the chances are high that at least some students are being intellectually challenged; however, some students might have lost the thread of the conversation. If the conversation is con-tinuing to deepen understanding, you should continue to listen, perhaps only restating some of the assertions to ensure that all participants are better able to follow the conversation. If the latter is the case, you need to determine whether to have the students probe the idea more deeply by asking them to evaluate their own thinking. Examples of probing ques-tions include, "Can you tell me what support you find for that idea?" or "How do you think this fits with the idea of happiness you developed ear-lier in the conversation?"

Alternately, it may be time to ask a question that moves the conver-sation to a different idea in the text. For example, during a seminar on the Preamble to the Constitution, students had been discussing the idea of freedom for more than 20 minutes. After all that time, they hadn't moved beyond restating in a variety of ways that freedom means that people can do whatever they want to do. To move the conversation, the facilitator asked: "How do you think *freedom* fits with *justice* in the Preamble?" This forced the participants to consider a new idea in light of their current conversation and provided the opportunity to add depth and nuance to the conversation up to that point.

As another example, during a seminar on Neil Postman's "My Graduation Speech," in which he divides the world into Athenians and Visigoths, the participants were discussing the relative merits of each with-out fully understanding Postman's definitions of either. The facilitator waited for a participant to draw others back to the text and ferret out more precisely what Postman meant. When this failed to happen, she redirected the seminar to a related, but different, question that required the participants to re-read a section of text before moving on.

Idea-Hopping

Another common developmental stage of learning the seminar process is when many students are participating but are jumping from idea to idea with few connections among statements. This idea-hopping is often tolerated by facilitators because it is easy to be so excited that students are talking about the text that we forget about the focus required. The result is a seminar with an extremely active discussion that doesn't result in a greater understanding of the text. The energy level can seem very high in such discussions, but a deep conversation of ideas generates its own energy—as well as understanding.

One group of students had several months of idea-hopping seminars that seemed, on the surface, to be lively conversations. But they and the facilitator always ended the seminar feeling less than satisfied. Finally, when discussing Alfred Lord Tennyson's poem, "Ulysses," the students probed every line of the text—even probing the phrase, "the utmost bound of human thought," for 15 minutes—and spent an hour building on one another's ideas. After the seminar, everyone left the room looking and feeling energized. A good seminar like this one is marked by reflective activity.

Challenging Ideas

Challenge is balanced when students begin to recognize that all interpretations of the text are not equal; some are more plausible than others, and it is the students' role to discuss the most plausible and reject the least plausible. It is sometimes said that there are no right or wrong ideas in a seminar. This is simply not true. There are gradations of plausibility or supportability. For example, an assertion that Langston Hughes's "Theme for English B" was the lamentation of a frustrated woman is simply unsupportable. An assertion that Hughes was attempting to convey his frustration with the grading system at his school is certainly not the most plausible interpretation of the text, but it is somewhat supportable and would be worthy of seminar discussion. An experienced seminar group should develop more plausible explanations and eventually abandon the least plausible. A group at this stage of seminar development is ready to become the primary driving force of their conversations.

The students in Ms. Milani's class continued to circle around "The Allegory of the Cave." Overall, the conversation was very respectful, and they had all agreed on a visual description of the Cave, but Ms. Milani could sense the group's frustration with still not "getting" the allegory. They hopped from one line to another—"what's up with the chains?" and "why would they just sit there and look at the shadows? . . ."

"OK," Thomas said. "I understand that the light outside the Cave, and not the shadows inside, is 'truth,' but I still don't see the point."

"Yeah, it's like he's telling us how it is, but not telling us why," said Georgia.

"What do you think about Socrates's comment in paragraph 15, that even people who are shown the light often return to the Cave only to be convinced by an 'instructor' that the shadows are reality?" Ms. Milani asked, trying to push the conversation deeper by heading it in a slightly different direction.

"That line makes no sense to me!" Tim exclaimed. "That was even more confusing." A short silence ensued while people pondered the section.

"Well," Julie said, speaking for the first time, "it's kind of like Socrates is pointing out that even when we have the opportunity to see truth, it is difficult to continue to look. Since most people see shadows as truth, most people will just go back to thinking like they always have."

"Yeah," said Rob. "It's like peer pressure will keep you from trying to learn the real truth. People might think you are crazy." The conversation began to build quickly with those two windows into its meaning. The group started to relate the Cave to life itself instead of bouncing from one line to another. Afterward, everyone talked about how their understanding of the allegory had changed enormously during the group's conversation.

5 Ownership

Discussion is lively and focused on understanding ideas in the text. Students are asking most of the critical questions.

Dictatorship   **Anarchy**

Indicators:
- Frustrated students
- Facilitator-centered conversation
- Intellectually weak seminar

Ownership

Indicators:
- Undisciplined argumentation
- Debates marked by righteous indignation
- Students left out of conversation

When Ms. Finn's seminar on the "To Be or Not to Be" soliloquy from Hamlet began, her students dove into the text. They politely said, "I disagree with your point," probed different ideas in the text, and obviously wanted to struggle with difficult issues in the text. Safety, authentic participation, and challenge were comfortably balanced in this classroom. But something was missing. The students weren't really talking to each other. Ms. Finn asked a question, a few students answered, and on at least three occasions, other students began to delve further into the ideas.

However, just as everyone seemed engaged, Ms. Finn would go back to her prepared list of questions and offer another one. They were open and challenging questions, but the conversation was not open for long before it moved on to something else. The moving on was always a result of Ms. Finn's next question, rather than a student question or comment. At one point, the students started to talk about something in depth, and Ms. Finn broke in at a pause to ask her next question. The students looked at her in a funny way because her question had nothing to do with their current conversation, but they dutifully attempted to answer her new question. It seemed like she should be sitting in the center of the circle.

Ownership is perhaps the most difficult fulcrum to maintain in balance, particularly for the inexperienced facilitator. However, a quality of all successful seminar discussions is that the students feel they have ownership of the ideas explored and generated. The students should be driving the conversation and doing the intellectual "heavy lifting"[1] during the seminar. In a successful, student-driven seminar, students shoulder the primary load in working to understand the ideas in the text by asking questions, supporting their assertions with direct textual references, and making observations. This doesn't mean that students do all of the talking; rather, it means that they are doing most of the analysis and evaluation. This is difficult for facilitators. When the discussion is silent or slow moving, you must consider whether to ask another question of your own or wait for students to find a solid foothold in the text to begin their climb toward better understanding. On the other end of the spectrum, if there is a great deal of student discussion about the text, you must focus on the depth and quality of the discussion. Although this fulcrum is related to authentic participation and challenge, it is focused more on decreasing the facilitator focus of the seminar while increasing the quality of the discussion. It is listed last because it is the most advanced fulcrum to learn to balance.

RECOGNIZING OWNERSHIP ISSUES

Questions to consider in determining whether an issue is related to ownership include:

- Who is asking the most critical questions?
- Who is determining the direction of the seminar?
- Who is taking primary responsibility for the integrity of the conversation?

The answer to all of the above questions should be the students. Until the correct balance has been established in safety, authentic participation, and challenge, the facilitator will have to remain a driving force, perhaps covertly so, in the seminar. To extend the driving analogy, the facilitator should have a steering wheel, gas pedal, and brake and should be ready to use them as necessary. Knowing how often and when to use them is the key to facilitation.

Avoiding Anarchy

If the group isn't ready to drive the seminar while the facilitator sits back to enjoy the ride, anarchy can ensue. Instead of a respectful discussion, the talk sounds more like an argument or a series of interruptions, and several students check out of the conversation. A subtler version of anarchy sometimes happens with more experienced seminar groups when the facilitator assumes that participants don't really need assistance. In this case, the facilitator asks the opening question and then rarely or never speaks for the rest of the seminar. This hands-off approach is OK if students really are carrying the whole conversation themselves, but the facilitator should be constantly considering whether the group needs any intervention or support to help them reach a deeper understanding. If the group's members are ready to focus on driving by themselves, then the facilitator must be ready to give up the wheel.

Once the other three fulcrums are established, a seminar will become student driven if the facilitator can relinquish some direct control comfortably—in other words, if the facilitator is more willing to be the driver's education teacher in the seat next to the students driving the conversation. Some facilitators don't trust themselves and/or their students enough to "go with the flow" of the conversation, even if it has veered far from what the facilitator had envisioned. Those facilitators, like Ms. Finn, want to ask each of their questions in the order they had planned. As long as the conversation is still on the text, however, unexpected directions are OK. If the facilitator is doing everything right in terms of having students reflect on how they are having the conversation, they will self-regulate most of the conversation (remind each other when they're off text, or ask for further clarification, etc.). The facilitator then plays the role of a synthesizer, re-stater, and occasional provocateur, not primary pilot of the conversation.

Facilitator Releasing Control

Becoming the secondary driver and relinquishing direct control of the seminar can be difficult for some facilitators. There are two primary reasons for this difficulty: Facilitators may have trouble with any activity in which they are not the primary focus; or facilitators may be wedded to a particular line of inquiry for students to explore. An unwillingness to relinquish control is a philosophical and psychological issue beyond the scope of this book. The single piece of advice we offer here is to trust the seminar process. Students have interesting, marvelous ideas to share if you set up an environment that encourages them to share those ideas.

The other issue—forcing students to develop a particular argument or reach a particular understanding—is a mistake made by even the most experienced seminar leaders. As in Ms. Finn's *Hamlet* discussion, this tactic is often the result of teachers' facilitating a text in which they have a personal investment. For example, one of the most experienced facilitators we know is a Civil War scholar. During a seminar on Lincoln's Gettysburg Address, his students eventually became frustrated because he kept disrupting the flow of the development of their seminar by returning the group to a specific question he wanted to explore. Although the question was certainly worthy of exploration in a seminar format, it was by no means the only or even most vital idea explored by Lincoln in this speech. The seminar worked only because the students were very experienced as participants and ultimately were able to wrest control of the discussion from the facilitator, but not until he had forced them into a discussion about an idea they didn't want or need to have.

Student-Driven Discussions

From the very first seminar, you must remind students that it is their conversation and that you are not looking for a particular interpretation of the text. As a group, the goal is to critically evaluate the ideas in the text. As previously discussed, challenging the ideas of others is critical to advancing understanding. In a student-driven seminar, students are challenging each other with questions and bringing up points discussed previously. At the end, no one may remember anything you did. This doesn't mean you didn't do anything. It means that you used the extra cockpit sparingly and so smoothly it went unnoticed.

In Mr. Hunter's sixth-grade math class, students were discussing M. C. Escher's "Relativity" lithograph. Members of this experienced seminar group were asking each other questions, disagreeing with each others' ideas while referring back to the text, and probing deeper and deeper into the work. During the conversation, students had gone from simply noticing interesting details to trying to figure out how it all fit together. A student who loved the outdoors noted the difference between life inside the building and life outside, some students wondered about its symmetry, and one student challenged the class to find all of the geometric elements in the piece.

Mr. Hunter wondered when he should jump in with a question. He asked what they thought the mood of the painting was and how Escher used shapes to communicate mood. The group briefly addressed his question and then started talking about how the piece might represent life and death. He decided not to re-ask his question because the group was exploring new territory and getting a deeper understanding of the text, even if students weren't answering his question.

After the seminar, he asked the group what they had done well, and they said that they had done a good job following up each others' points and agreeing to disagree about a few things. They also said that they had a much better understanding of the text. Isaiah then said, "I appreciated how you let us talk for long periods of time without jumping in, but then would ask a question occasionally to get us to think about something we hadn't thought about yet. I know we didn't always answer your question."

"Is that OK?" asked Leslie. Mr. Hunter replied, "Well, it was fine with me because you were engaging in your own questions and answers. And you usually came back to my question eventually when you wanted to address it." Mary added, "I liked knowing that you were there to guide the conversation. It made me feel more willing to jump in."

NOTE

1. This is a term introduced to us by Eileen Landay, a colleague and teacher educator at Brown University.

6 The Facilitator Decision-Making Model

Although we have thus far discussed the fulcrums one at a time and suggested some ideas for balancing the fulcrums during a seminar, in practice, facilitating a seminar is not that straightforward. Regardless of the participants' and facilitator's experience with the seminar process, any of the fulcrums can be out of balance at any time. Ownership can be at the root of an issue during a group's first seminar, and safety can be a problem with a veteran group. Sometimes, multiple fulcrums are out of balance simultaneously. And sometimes, it is clear a seminar is not going well but less clear which fulcrum is the primary problem.

STEPS OF THE DECISION-MAKING PROCESS

Returning to the decision-making model we mentioned at the beginning of this section, in this chapter, we describe and illustrate the decision-making steps used by an effective facilitator. This framework breaks down the process of deciding what to do next as a facilitator into multiple steps:

1. Identify the issue

2. Identify possible causes

3. Match to primary fulcrum

4. Identify and apply possible strategies

5. Determine effectiveness and next steps

Of course, real decision making is messier than what we can capture here, and it happens much more quickly than the pace we take in the next few pages. However, we find that having a systematic way to apply the fulcrums helps facilitators make decisions that improve their seminars. As you practice using this framework, you will find it easier to balance the fulcrums and help your students gain a deeper understanding of the text, themselves, and each other.

Identifying the Issue

The first step is to determine whether an issue exists during your seminar by asking the question: What, if anything, is preventing students from coming to a deeper understanding of the text, themselves, and each other? There may, in fact, be numerous answers to this question. The challenge is to decide which issue is primary at this particular moment in a seminar. Identifying the issue is the key because you have to know what to address before you can decide how to address it most effectively. Often, you won't fully understand the issue when you begin to think about it, but you'll notice some indicator of a problem—students are talking in side conversations instead of to the whole group, or no one's referring to the text, or one student is being rude, for example. You start with this indicator and then move on to the next step in the decision-making model.

Identifying Possible Causes

Once you have identified the issue, you determine the possible causes of that issue. Any given issue can have multiple possible causes. For example, you decide that the issue is that very few students are talking. Why? Possible causes might be (1) the climate is unsafe—students are afraid to risk an idea; (2) students are not prepared; (3) the question is too difficult; (4) you're dominating as a facilitator, and students are relying on you to ask another question rather than offering their own question or statement. After determining the possibilities, you then decide which cause you think is relevant at this moment of the seminar. For the purpose of illustration, we will take you through the application of this model for each of the above four causes of very few students talking.

Matching to Primary Fulcrum

The next step is to take the cause you have identified and match it to the appropriate fulcrum. You must ask: Through which fulcrum is the cause best understood? In the example above, if you decide that students are quiet because students are afraid to risk an idea, you would match that with safety.

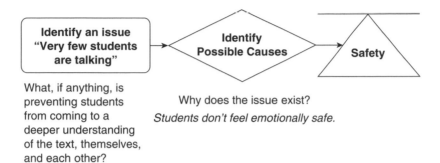

Identify an issue
"Very few students are talking"

What, if anything, is preventing students from coming to a deeper understanding of the text, themselves, and each other?

Identify Possible Causes

Why does the issue exist?
Students don't feel emotionally safe.

Safety

If you decide that students are quiet because they do not understand how to interact with one another, then the primary fulcrum would be authentic participation.

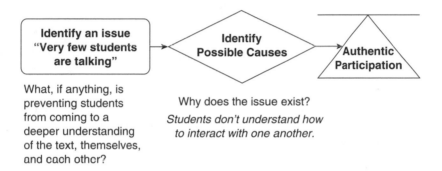

Identify an issue
"Very few students are talking"

What, if anything, is preventing students from coming to a deeper understanding of the text, themselves, and each other?

Identify Possible Causes

Why does the issue exist?
Students don't understand how to interact with one another.

Authentic Participation

Another possibility for silent students is that the question is too complex, and the students do not yet have the depth of understanding to address the question at this point in the seminar. If you determine this to be the case, then the primary fulcrum would be challenge.

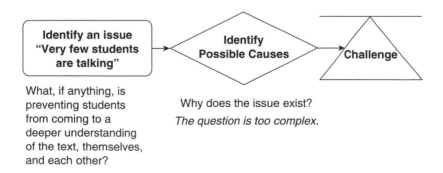

Identify an issue
"Very few students are talking"

What, if anything, is preventing students from coming to a deeper understanding of the text, themselves, and each other?

Identify Possible Causes

Why does the issue exist?
The question is too complex.

Challenge

If, however, you decide that students are quiet because you're dominating as a facilitator, and students are relying on you to ask another question, you would match that with the ownership fulcrum.

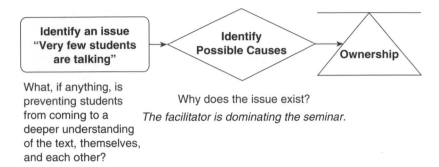

This process of matching to the primary fulcrum helps determine the scope of what you are trying to balance. The next step is to identify the possible strategies you might employ to achieve that balance.

Identifying and Applying Possible Strategies

Once you have determined the fulcrum, you ask: With which end of the fulcrum does the issue align? For example, you have already decided that students are quiet because they're afraid to risk an idea, which is a safety issue. Because the majority of students are quiet, you decide that it's an issue of tiptoeing. Now, you consider a range of strategies that you might use to address tiptoeing (see Part III, Chapter 8, for possible strategies), and you choose a strategy to apply to this seminar. For example, you might use a pair-share strategy: allowing students to work in pairs to answer a question and asking each pair to share their answer with the whole group. This strategy allows students to share an answer about which they may be unsure with one person before sharing it publicly. Most students (and adults) are much more comfortable sharing an idea with one peer than they are sharing with a whole group. This strategy can be used to combat certain types of safety issues at any point in a seminar.

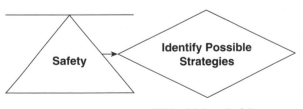

With which end of the
fulcrum does the issue align?

Tiptoeing: Pair-Share

If you decide students simply don't understand how they are supposed to interact with one another, then it is an authentic participation issue, and silent students are the result of the nonparticipation end of the fulcrum. A strategy that can be applied is to call a time-out in the seminar. By calling literally calling "time," you are preserving the seminar for conversation about ideas. Clearly demarcating time to talk about process as outside the seminar time helps students understand the boundaries of the seminar. Once time is called, you may then review once more the types of participation that are appropriate for a seminar. You might even simulate and model a seminar conversation. For example, you could ask a question and, once someone answers, you could ask the students what might happen next. When someone else adds a statement, you might remind them that the next person might want to agree or disagree with one of the previous statements and provide support for their answer with the text. After 5 or 10 minutes of deliberately demonstrating the types of interactions that should be occurring, ask students if they are ready, call time-in, and ask another open-ended question.

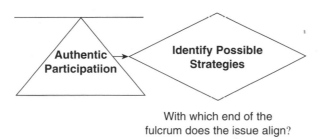

With which end of the
fulcrum does the issue align?

Nonparticipation: Time-out—Review and Check for Preparation

Another reason students may be silent is that the question is too difficult. This is an indication of a challenge issue on the Rosetta stone end of the fulcrum. The first strategy to apply in this case is to ask a less difficult question. For example, if your question about what the shadows on the wall represent is met with blank stares in a seminar on Plato's Allegory of the Cave, consider what ideas students might need to address prior to discussing that question. Assuming the students have an understanding of the literal interpretation of the Cave, an alternative question might be, "What do you think are the critical elements of the Cave?" This question will elicit a variety of answers and allow students to collaboratively develop a sense of the Cave and begin developing the foundation for building theories on the meaning of the allegory.

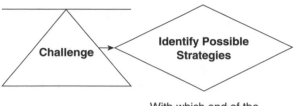

With which end of the
fulcrum does the issue align?

Rosetta stone: Ask a less difficult question.

Finally, students might be silent because the facilitator is dominating the conversation and not allowing students to participate or to pursue student-generated lines of thinking. For example, students have developed an interesting and appropriate discussion of the meaning of justice in the context of the Preamble to the Constitution, and just as they seem ready to take the idea in a new direction, you ask a question relating to the concept of welfare without suggesting the students link the two ideas. If this happens once, students may jump right into the next question; however, eventually, students may decide to stop participating because they feel that they are merely answering a series of teacher-generated questions and are not engaged in an organic conversation driven by the ideas in the text and discussion. To return to our analogy from Chapter 5, they know how to drive, but they haven't been given the steering wheel. If you suspect that ownership is the primary fulcrum and that the problem is at the dictatorship end of the spectrum, then a possible strategy is to ask the students for questions they may have about the text or ideas from the conversation. Then, you allow the students to follow up and take over driving the seminar for awhile, at least until another issue develops.

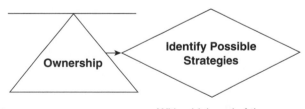

With which end of the
fulcrum does the issue align?

Dictatorship: Ask for student questions and let students follow up.

Determining Effectiveness of Strategy and Next Steps

After identifying an issue, a possible cause, and a fulcrum, and applying a strategy, you must then ask the question: Does the issue remain? If your answer is yes, then you have two choices: (1) Try another strategy and (2) reassess the cause of the issue. For example, after your pair-share strategy to address tiptoeing, allow a few minutes before deciding whether or not the seminar is still quiet. If yes, then try another strategy such as role playing. If that's ineffective, then re-assess the cause. Perhaps there is a different reason students are being quiet. If your answer is no to the question of whether the seminar is still quiet, then return to the first step in the process, which is to ask what, if anything, is preventing students from coming to a deeper understanding of the text, themselves, and each other. Begin the seminar decision-making process again, looking for anything else that is hindering the success of a seminar.

The figure below represents the decision-making model and examples we've just described.

Facilitator asks: What if anything is preventing students from coming to a deeper understanding of the text, themselves, and each other?

Identify an Issue:
Very few students are talking

Identify Possible Causes:
Why does the issue exist?

Students don't feel emotionally safe	Students don't understand how to interact with one another	The question is too difficult	The facilitator is dominating the seminar

Through which fulcrum is the cause best understood?

Safety	Authentic Participation	Challenge	Ownership

With which end of the fulcrum does the issue align?
Identify possible strategies

Tiptoeing	Nonparticipation	Rosetta stone	Dictatorship
Pair-Share	*Time-out/role-play*	*A simpler question*	*Relinquish wheel*

Assess Effectiveness of Strategy/Determine Next Steps
Does the issue remain?

If yes, try another strategy for that fulcrum

If yes again, reconsider the cause

If no, return to beginning question

This model can be applied to any issue that arises during a seminar. Expert facilitators often make decisions quickly and perhaps less cleanly than this model suggests. Like any model of human decision making, this one is not perfect, and understanding the model will not make you an expert facilitator. With consistent practice, however, you will begin to internalize the structure and become better at making decisions at each step.

PART III

Improving Student-Centered Discussions

N ow that you understand the fulcrum framework, you should be ready to apply the fulcrums to your own facilitation. The only trick is, once you have identified that a discussion is not balanced in one or more of the fulcrum areas, what do you do about it? In this section, we summarize strategies to help you balance safety, authentic participation, challenge, and ownership in the discussions you're facilitating. Chapter 7 includes strategies that apply to ongoing improvement across all the fulcrums. Chapter 8 includes strategies specific to each fulcrum. We have tried all of these techniques in our own discussions, and our collection of strategies continues to grow as we continue to develop as facilitators.

7 Strategies for Ongoing Improvement Across All the Fulcrums

Each of the following strategies is broad and can be applied in a variety of situations. You can use the strategies for general feedback and assessment of the strengths and needs of your discussion. You can also apply them more specifically to focus on a particular fulcrum. Some of the strategies focus on involving students in the process of improving discussions; other strategies focus on the facilitator and what you can do on your own and with colleagues to improve discussions.

REFLECTION

Develop the habit and skill of reflecting at a metacognitive level about the seminar process. In our experience, nothing improves seminars faster than having an ongoing conversation before and after the seminar about *how* the process did happen, should happen, and could happen. Time is our most precious and scarce resource in schools, so it is easy to omit this step due to time constraints. You will find it far more valuable, however, to cut the seminar a few minutes short to allow participants to reflect on what's been done. This habit of reflection is necessary for both participants and the facilitator.

What It Looks Like for Participants

• *Pre-seminar:* Set goals as a whole group and as individuals. Before a seminar, ask participants to set an individual goal for themselves based on their last seminar. Give them some examples of goals they might set. For example, a quiet participant who did not speak in the last seminar might set a goal of speaking at least once. Or a talkative participant who dominated the last seminar might set a goal of limiting talking. While the participants write their goals down, you should write down a goal for yourself. As a facilitator, you might set a goal of focusing on safety because the last seminar you led with this group had disrespectful behavior and comments. Or, you might focus on asking follow-up questions because you think this class is ready to be pushed more deeply into the text. Then, ask group members what they should work on as a group today based on their last seminar. Get ideas from the participants, and then agree on one area to focus on for today's seminar. A group might decide to focus on speaking one at a time because they all interrupted each other during the last seminar. Or, the group might focus on building on each others' ideas because they tended to just put forth their individual thoughts in the last seminar.

Examples of Goals for Individuals and Groups

For an individual participant:

- *Listen more closely*
- *Ask a question*
- *Try not to talk so much, OR don't talk more than three times*
- *Speak at least once*
- *Refer to the text when I speak*
- *Respect my peers and not laugh at or make fun of comments they make*

For a group:

- *Speak one at a time—no interrupting*
- *No side conversations (talking to peers sitting near you while seminar happens around you)*
- *Be respectful: No rude comments or laughing at people*
- *Refer to the text*
- *Use each others' names as a sign of respect*
- *Build on each others' ideas*
- *Understand the text more deeply by the end of seminar*
- *Allow silence for people to think*
- *Try to balance opportunities to speak so that more people can speak and no one dominates the conversation*
- *Stay on the text; don't let the conversation stray*

- *Post-seminar:* Reflect and debrief so participants can see how well they met the goals they set before the seminar. Ask participants to return to their goal and write how they did in meeting that goal. Ask if anyone wants to share his or her goal and performance. Then, focus on how you did as a group. Ask students what they did well as a group today in the seminar. Ask them what they could work on next time. Remind students of the goal the group set before the seminar, and ask how they think they did with it today. Ask them what they think they should work on next time. As facilitator, you should add any strengths and needs you noticed if students have not identified them.

What It Looks Like for a Facilitator

- As facilitator, you should also set goals for your facilitation, preferably based on previous seminars and what you know about the group of students whose discussion you will be facilitating. For your goals, you may choose a fulcrum that you're going to pay special attention to in the discussion, and try to articulate what specific elements of that fulcrum are critical for you as a facilitator and for the group of students having the discussion.

Examples of Goals for Facilitators

- *Focus on safety—allow no disrespectful comments*
- *Look down at my text—no eye contact with participants*
- *Help students refer to the text by asking them to point out the place in the text that supports their idea*
- *Ask follow-up questions to probe for deeper thinking*
- *Allow wait time; don't fill silence with a question right away*
- *Be neutral—no positive reinforcement; no nodding, "great idea" comments, or other indications of my opinion of the conversation and individual ideas*
- *Mapping: Focus on keeping track of the conversation in writing as a tool for me*
- *Listen carefully to students' conversation, and be ready to go a different direction than I planned; don't be afraid to ask a question that's not on my prepared list*

- After the seminar, reflect on how you did with your goal(s), and make notes to yourself about what you want to focus on in your next discussion. The Facilitator Reflection Form can also be helpful with this process.

Facilitator Reflection Form

Reflect on the discussion and make a short statement about each fulcrum (for your primary fulcrum focus, you may want a more detailed description). You should consult your seminar map, notes, and any assessments (e.g., Fulcrum-Based Seminar Rubric) associated with the seminar.

Safety *is in balance when many students are participating and there are no side conversations, sarcasm, or teasing. How was safety today?*

Authentic Participation *is in balance when student comments refer directly to the text or to another participant's comments and are made in a respectful manner. How was authentic participation today?*

Challenge *is in balance when student comments address the complexities of the text's ideas and deepen understanding. How was challenge today?*

Ownership *is in balance when discussion is lively and focused on understanding ideas in the text; students are asking most of the critical questions. How was ownership today?*

Identify a moment in the seminar in which you felt a fulcrum was either out of balance or in balance. Briefly describe this moment. Be sure to include enough detail to help you remember the moment when you read this in the future.

If you chose an out-of-balance moment, which strategies did you try or would you like to try in the future? If you chose an in-balance moment, what were you doing in seminar that contributed most to the balance?

What modifications would you make to this plan for future seminars (pre-seminar, questions, etc.)?

Note two elements that can be particularly helpful:

1. Focus on a particular moment in the discussion, rather than spending all your time thinking about the whole discussion. This focus on a particular moment can help you think deeply about one element, which can make it easier to think about improvement. For example, in the vignette in Chapter 4, a moment to focus on might be when William voices his lack of a clear picture of "the Cave."

2. Jot notes for adjustments you would make to your discussion plan. We never quite want to do this after a seminar because we're busy preparing our next lessons for students, but we thank ourselves later if we make the time for a few quick notes on what we would do next time. Examples include: ask a different question (often one we or a student asked during the discussion that wasn't on our plan); do a different preparation before the seminar to get students ready; choose a different text because this one just didn't work.

Variation: Envisioning

Either on your own or with a colleague, generate statements describing each fulcrum when balanced. What does it look like? What does it sound like? What are the students doing? What type of language are they using? How are they relating to the text? What are students not doing? What is the facilitator doing? What isn't the facilitator doing? Sometimes, envisioning a balanced seminar can help in thinking about what strategies you would need to use to get your own seminar in balance.

SEMINAR MAPPING

Mapping will help you keep track of both the process and the content of the conversation during a seminar. Like any system of taking notes, each facilitator has a different style for mapping. You will develop your own as you practice mapping and decide what sorts of information you want to keep track of. Most people find it very difficult to map and facilitate simultaneously when they are first learning to facilitate. As you learn, it's helpful to have a colleague map for you, if possible. Otherwise, start by just noting one or two things on your map and build your skills gradually.

What It Looks Like

- *Content:* Note questions and comments participants make; you can follow up on these later if you wish.
- *Process:* Note behaviors like questioning, referring to text, following up on another person's idea, having a side conversation, interrupting, acting disrespectfully, and so on. You might also note who is

talking and how often, as well as who is not talking; you can then use strategies to encourage whatever behaviors you'd like to see but aren't seeing, such as referring to text or drawing quieter people into the conversation.

- *Generally:* You can use your map after the seminar to assess how the conversation went and which fulcrums you might need to focus on.
- Do your map on an overhead transparency, and show the overhead to students after the seminar as you debrief. Students love to see the map, and it can be a helpful tool for reflection purposes.

Here are two examples of different seminar maps. Both authors write all student names in the circle according to how students are seated. Both authors also note some student comments so that they can return to them later in the conversation or ask a follow-up question.

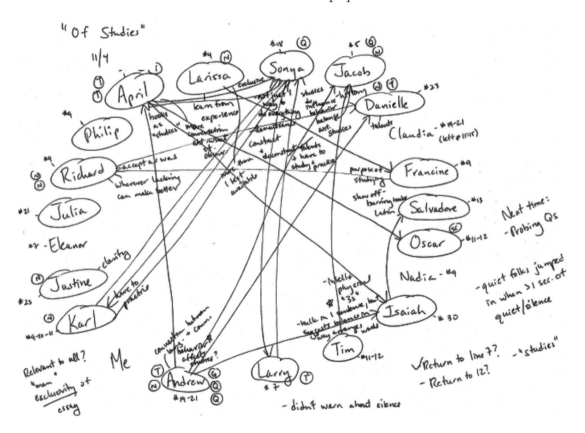

Liz's style:

- Circle the names of participants once they have spoken so that she can tell with a quick glance who has and who hasn't yet spoken. If she uses a round-robin style response for the opening question, Liz starts circling after the round-robin is over.

- Draw arrows when a participant responds to or asks a question of a peer so that she can see how much exchange and building of ideas there is and where that happens—is it only between two or three people, or is it fairly evenly distributed? If participants are idea-hopping or are very quiet, she will have few arrows and will have a better sense of what area she needs to try to address with her next question.
- Use a *Q* or a *?* to denote students' asking a question.
- Use a *T* to denote students' referring to text.
- Write comments from the opening question around the outside of the circle. Write comments from the rest of the seminar on the inside of the circle. Put a * next to or circle comments to return to later.
- Use *SC* to denote side conversation.
- Write notes about student behavior next to student's name.
- Write questions or ideas she thinks of while listening (either process or content related) somewhere on the bottom so that she can refer to them later.
- Doodle or go over existing circles when trying very hard to have wait time and not make eye contact.

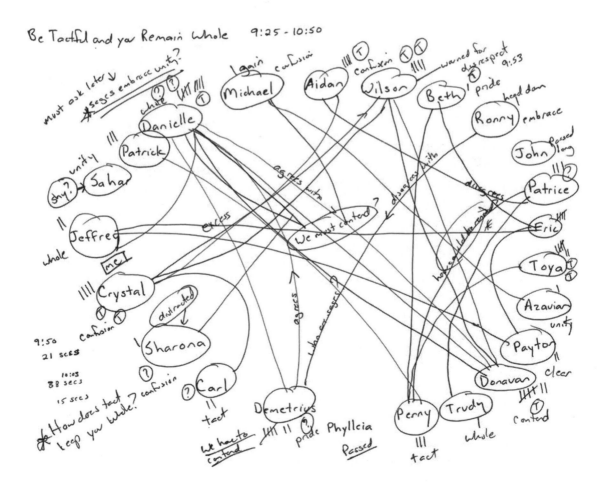

Mike's style (comments only pertain to differences from the Liz example):

- Write comments regarding the nature of responses from one participant to another (e.g., *agrees with*).
- Write the length of long silences.
- Tally the number of times each person speaks.
- Note significant statements for reference later in discussion.

TEACHING THE FULCRUMS TO STUDENTS

We've found that when we include students in the process of improving seminars, our seminars improve more quickly and with longer-lasting results. The conversation, after all, is theirs, so improving the conversation should be, at least in part, their task as well. Enlisting students' help accomplishes several things that support improvement: increases students' awareness of what a seminar should look and feel like, provides language for discussing seminar development and analysis, and demonstrates that everyone is responsible for a good conversation, not just the facilitator.

What It Looks Like

- Before sharing the fulcrums with students, ask them what makes a good seminar. Brainstorm the characteristics of a good seminar, and then draw on those characteristics to explain the fulcrums.
- Show students the Fulcrum-Based Seminar Rubric (see Resource B). Describe the fulcrums, and use the rubric when debriefing after a seminar. Watching a videotape of a seminar (either their own or someone else's) and applying the rubric to the videotape can make it easier to get everyone on the same page about what each part of the rubric means.
- Share the fulcrum categories with students and have them make their own Fulcrum-Based Seminar Rubric—what does it look like when safety, authentic participation, challenge, and ownership are in balance? What does it look like when they're not in balance?
- Use the language of the fulcrums when setting goals and debriefing the discussion with students: "How did we do with safety today? How can we improve next time?"

FISHBOWL

Sometimes, it helps to have half the students focus on reflecting on the seminar process while the other half focuses on participating in the discussion itself. Although some teachers choose to conduct all their seminars with this two-circle method, we advise using the fishbowl technique as a tool to focus on specific issues rather than as a general procedure. We prefer to have all students participate in the seminar unless the group is too large to have a conversation together (more than 35 students, in our experience) or needs help focusing on specific seminar behaviors (particularly safety). Otherwise, setting individual and group goals before the seminar and debriefing those goals afterward generally suffices for reflecting on process. That said, the fishbowl is a great technique for in-depth reflection and can achieve some of the same goals as videotape, if you do not have access to video.

What It Looks Like

• Instead of the single circle you usually use for a seminar, set up two circles, one inside the other. Participants in the outer circle have individual tasks, which you distribute on file cards. Participants in the inner circle have the seminar text for the day. As facilitator, you sit in the inside circle. Ask for a volunteer timekeeper, and have that student notify you when 15 to 20 minutes have passed (this time can be adjusted based on the length of your class). During the 15 to 20 minutes, only people in the inside circle can speak as they have a seminar. People in the outside circle must observe according to their designated task. After the timekeeper calls time, you go around the outer circle. Now, only people in the outer circle can talk. They each read their task, and tell the group what they observed. After you have gone around the outer circle, the participants switch circles, so that the outer circle becomes the inner circle and vice versa. Repeat the process.

• The seminar conversation should pick up where the other conversation left off. You do not need to start over from the beginning of the seminar. Generally, the second half of a seminar delves more deeply into the text and has better balance of the fulcrums as students take more ownership of helping achieve that balance. The process of debriefing individual observations around the outer circle makes specific seminar behaviors and patterns visible, which thus makes it easier to address those issues.

Tasks

We highly recommend making a set of index cards with tasks and laminating them so that you will have them on hand for a variety of uses. It's a good idea to have at least one or two of the tasks directly related to you, the facilitator. Students love the role of watching you and telling about your behaviors. In addition, ownership becomes more shared when everybody is part of the growing and improving process, and you can get valuable feedback on your facilitation. Also, it's OK to have more than one person doing the same task. The group will get a wider interpretation of its participation, the feedback can be more focused on a few things, and it's less confusing for the participants to make sense of the feedback.

Examples of Observation Tasks

- Count how many times each person speaks. Who speaks the most? Who doesn't speak at all?
- What kinds of body language do you see?
- Watch the facilitator—is he or she talking too much? too little?
- Which questions or comments are not addressed?
- Make counterarguments.
- Watch eye contact. Where are the participants looking—at the facilitator or at each other?
- Whom do the speakers address—the facilitator or each other?
- What part of the text does the discussion ignore?
- Compare how many times boys and girls speak. Of the two groups, who speaks for a longer period of time? Do the groups differ in how they speak?
- Watch the quiet people. Are they listening? How do you know? Do they look like they want to talk?
- Summarize the content of the discussion.
- Write down all questions that are asked. Who asks them?
- Watch the person opposite you (facing you) in the inner circle. What do you observe about that person's participation, body language, and so on?
- Time the periods of silence. What is the longest period of silence? Does it look like people are thinking during silence? are confused, or bored, or what? Why do you think they're quiet?
- Count interruptions and side conversations.
- Count how many times we refer to the text.
- Count how many times we digress from the text.
- Watch the facilitator—is he or she making eye contact with the participants? Is she or he giving them positive reinforcement, or is she or he neutral?
- Count how many times somebody responds to or builds on another person's point. Do you think people are generally connecting to other participants' points, or are they ignoring others' ideas?
- Watch the outer circle. Are people listening to the inner circle? Daydreaming? Do people seem engaged in what's happening?

Make sure the tasks address whatever fulcrum you're focusing on. If you're focusing on safety, for example, you might focus on things like counting how often each person speaks, body language, boys' versus girls' talk time, quiet people, and eye contact. If you're focusing on challenge, however, you might use things like the content of the discussion, questions asked, counterarguments, ignored parts of the text, and so on.

SEMINAR FOLDERS

A seminar folder is a wonderful tool for both you and the participants to track your development in the seminar process over time. It's a good idea to keep all seminar folders in a file drawer in the classroom so that students have access to them and don't lose them. Having student seminar work together in a folder is also handy for conferences with parents so that you can show them what students are doing in class seminars.

What It Looks Like for Participants

- Keep all seminar texts, and any pre- and post-seminar work in the folder.
- Fill out a running reflection tool about personal goals and keep it in the folder. Use this tool to help set goals before each seminar.
- Sample tool (we put three of these per side on paper, front and back, so students can easily look back to their goals and reflections from previous seminars).

Seminar text title: _____

Date: _____

Pre-seminar: My goal for today's seminar:

Post-seminar: How did I do with my goal today?

What should I focus on next seminar to make me a better participant?

What It Looks Like for a Facilitator

- Keep all seminar texts, Seminar Planning and Reflection Forms, Fulcrum-Based Seminar Rubrics, and maps of seminars in a folder.
- Keep peer-coaching feedback and self-assessments (e.g., completed rubric) in this folder.
- Fill out a running reflection tool about personal goals and keep it in the folder. Use this tool to help set goals before each seminar.
- Sample tool (we put three of these per side on paper, front and back, so we can easily look back to our goals and reflections from previous seminars).

Seminar text title: _____

Date: _____

Pre-seminar: My goal for today's seminar:

Post-seminar: How did I do with my goal today?

What should I focus on next seminar to make me a better facilitator?

What It Looks Like for a Group

- Fill out a running reflection tool about group goals. You can either keep this in your folder, or post it in the room so that everyone can see it. You can also designate a student to be responsible for filling this out.

Seminar text title: _____

Date: _____

Pre-seminar: Our group goal for today's seminar:

Post-seminar: What did we do well as a group today?

What could we work on next time?

How did we do with our group goal today?

What should we focus on next seminar?

VIDEOTAPE

Videotape can be a valuable reflection tool for both you and your students. It allows you to see many of the things that are too difficult to keep track of during the seminar, and it does not lie. Although the group may think everyone did a good job talking one at a time, students may see on videotape that they interrupted each other 12 times during the seminar. One student we know was confident that he was a fabulous seminar participant because he talked a lot. When he watched the video, he suddenly realized that his habit of getting up and moving around during the seminar was highly disruptive and rude. Likewise, although you may think you're not making eye contact and positively reinforcing student comments, you might see that you're still looking at students and smiling when they talk. Here again, it will be tempting to think that the time taken to watch videotape of a seminar could be better spent on having a seminar or delving into some other aspect of the curriculum. However, used as an occasional tool, videotape will illuminate your and your students' seminar process and push you to have the skills necessary for deep conversation much more quickly than if you ignore this tool.

Video can be as general or as specific a tool as you like. You can simply show the video and look for general strengths and needs, or you can focus on a particular area.

What It Looks Like for Participants

- Show the video on a different day than the seminar. Show as much or as little of the video as necessary to achieve whatever you have set as your objective. Often, 5 to 10 minutes of the video will suffice.
- Focus students on their individual participation.
- Focus students on the group's participation.
- Be sure to focus on what the group is doing well in addition to what the group can improve.

What It Looks Like for the Facilitator

- Again, watch the video with a specific objective in mind. Are you looking for general strengths and needs in your facilitation, or are you looking at something specific, for example, when to challenge students for a deeper understanding?
- Compare the video to your map of the seminar. How accurately does your map reflect the seminar? Or, if it is still difficult for you to map during a seminar, map the seminar as you watch the video. This can be a great way to practice mapping. Again, you don't have to map the entire seminar, but try it for 15 minutes.
- Complete the Fulcrum-Based Seminar Rubric (see Resource B) as you watch the video. Which fulcrums are in balance? Which are not? What could you do next seminar to attain better balance?
- Be sure to focus on what you are doing well, in addition to what you can improve.

ASSESSMENT

Teachers often ask us if they can and should assess the seminar. The short answer is yes, you can and should assess the seminar, but you should not evaluate it. The longer answer is that you should think about all the ways students participate in a seminar (prepare, listen, think, speak, respect others and the text) and then consider which of those you can measure. During a seminar, it is difficult to measure how well students are listening or thinking. Sometimes, they look like they are thinking about the after-school basketball game, and then, they say something fairly brilliant that lets you know they were listening all along. Thus, your participation grade would be merely a speaking grade.

Also, in our experience, giving students a grade for speaking often leads to inauthentic participation as students speak just to get a high participation grade rather than to contribute to the conversation and understanding of the text. Giving a grade for participation also elevates speaking above the other prime seminar skills of listening and thinking, both of which we want to nurture. That said, you can measure how well students prepare for a seminar if you give them some sort of assignment beforehand to help get them ready to participate actively. A post-seminar assignment is also a good opportunity to measure what students were thinking about during the seminar, particularly a writing assignment that follows up on the seminar. You would assess these written assignments like any other work in your classroom.

You can, however, assess the seminar process in the true sense of assessment—that is, to identify areas of accomplishment and areas for future growth. The goal-setting and reflection piece before and after a seminar serves as self-assessment. If you would like to assess further, you can develop a rubric around the skills you would like to assess. One teacher we know developed a rubric with her students. Sometimes, students self-assess using the rubric. Other times, she completes the rubric for each student after a seminar based on her observations. Still other times, she asks a colleague to complete the rubric for each student while observing a seminar. She also gives a written comment or two for each student when she completes the rubric. She's an experienced seminar facilitator and can keep track of several things at once in a seminar. If you're just starting out, we recommend relying on student self-assessment and limiting teacher assessment to work done before and after the seminar.

What It Looks Like

- *Student self-assessment:* before- and after-seminar goal setting and reflection (see "Reflection" section in this chapter).
- *Pre-seminar preparation:* defining vocabulary words, answering questions about the text, marking up the text, and so on; assessed like other class work.
- *Post-seminar follow-up:* often a writing assignment; extends a seminar and gives you a window into what students are taking away from the seminar; assessed like other class work.

- *Rubric for the seminar:* developed with your class; includes categories related to the skills you want to focus on (e.g., decorum or respect, preparation, text reference, body language—eyes following the conversation, sitting up straight); can be used for student self-assessment, for teacher assessment, or for outsider's assessment (e.g., teacher colleague).

PEER PLANNING

A large part of your work as a facilitator happens before the seminar as you prepare the text and the questions you might ask. It can be very helpful to have a colleague or colleagues assist with this process. They might have other ideas for texts or questions that will better help you achieve your seminar goals.

What It Looks Like

- You and a colleague select a text and plan a seminar together. You both lead seminars on that text. Afterward, you debrief how it went and make notes about what you might do differently next time.
- *Variation:* Only one of you leads a seminar on that text. However, the process of planning with someone else is helpful for all teachers in terms of developing the skills of writing good questions and selecting good texts, even if you don't all use that seminar plan in your classrooms.
- You and several colleagues select a text and plan a seminar together. As a team or as a school, you have a schoolwide or teamwide seminar on the same text: On the same day, each participating faculty member leads a seminar on the same text using the same base plan (actual questions will vary according to the different seminars, but everyone starts with the same plan). This serves the double purpose of having the students discuss a common text, which can be a powerful experience for a community, and of having faculty facilitate with a common text and plan, which can make it easier to debrief and improve seminars as a group.
- You select the text and plan questions, and then show it to a colleague for feedback before a seminar.

PEER COACHING

Watch and be watched: As with the videotape, getting another perspective on facilitation can be invaluable in your development as a facilitator.

Coaching can be as general or as specific as you like. However, in our experience, if you have a specific focus, such as authentic participation, you will learn more from the peer coaching. The more specific your focus, the more specific the feedback you will get. Often, you learn as much or more from watching as from being watched, so be sure to do both.

What It Looks Like

- *Watching:* You'll develop your own system for watching based on what you and the colleague you're watching are interested in. We generally prefer to use either the Fulcrum-Based Seminar Rubric or a two-column format when observing colleagues. In the two-column format, the first column is notes about factual observations of what we see, with evidence, and the second column is our reactions, questions, and judgments about what we see.

What I See	What I Think/Wonder

Of course, this is not an evaluative process—it's an assessment designed to be helpful to both the observer and the observed. You and your colleague should carve out time for a debriefing after the observation so you can share your thoughts about the seminar process.

- *Being watched:* Frame a question or focus area based on your goals/objectives. Ask your colleague to watch specifically for that question or focus. Be sure to debrief after the observation, including strategies for improving future seminars.
- Have a colleague map a seminar while you facilitate (or vice versa), and then debrief after the seminar.
- *Variation: Modeling.* Ask an experienced facilitator to do a demonstration seminar in your class. This strategy is especially effective if you are just learning the seminar process but can also be effective for modeling a specific issue, such as how to relinquish strict teacher

control in the seminar or how to ask probing questions. Many teachers we know appreciate the opportunity to see an experienced facilitator work with their own students so that they can see what a discussion might look like in their own classroom.

CASE STUDY

Digging deeply into a specific moment of the seminar can help you think concretely about your facilitation and about what strategies to use for improvement. You can do this strategy on your own as a reflection, but ideally, you'll have colleagues help you think through it. Using a protocol like the one we suggest below to guide the conversation helps to structure the conversation and give everyone a chance to share their ideas.

What It Looks Like

- Write about a specific moment during a seminar when you thought one of the fulcrums was out of balance or in balance. Include as much detail as you can about what students were saying and doing and what you were saying and doing. Have two colleagues do the same, and bring your text and seminar plan with write-up (your case study) to a meeting with your colleagues. You can do this with any number of people, but we like three because that means you get two people responding to each case study, which provides a wider range of ideas than a single partner would, and everyone in the group can share a case study during one planning period.
- One person shares a case study [3 minutes].
- The other participants ask any clarifying questions they need answers to in order to be able to think about the case [2 minutes].
- Then the participants discuss which fulcrums they think were in or out of balance and discuss the decisions the facilitator should consider, as well as possible strategies the facilitator could try. During this piece, the case presenter doesn't speak and takes notes [5 minutes].
- Finally, the case presenter responds to what has been said and describes planned activities for the next seminar [3 minutes].
- Continue with the other participants sharing their case studies one at a time.
- If there is time at the end, the group should take a couple of minutes to brainstorm challenges, decisions, or strategies they shared. If you were doing this as part of a larger group, the whole group could then debrief, making a list of common challenges, decisions, and strategies.

8 Strategies for Improving Specific Fulcrums

I n this chapter, you'll find strategies to help with each fulcrum. Many of the strategies are quite straightforward and do not take long to implement. If you are using this section to solve a particular issue that has arisen in your discussions, you can go straight to that part of the chapter. For example, if you think you're having a safety issue on the attacking personalities end of the fulcrum, you'll go to that section, where you'll find several strategies to try.

SAFETY ISSUES: ATTACKING PERSONALITIES

For a "Jerry Springer" attacking personalities environment, you can use several strategies.

Seminar Ground Rules

Be sure to firmly establish seminar ground rules, and post them in the room. Review them before every seminar as a reminder, even with experienced participants who usually adhere to the guidelines.

What It Looks Like

Make a poster with the following ground rules for participants:

- Prepare
- Participate

- Listen
- Think
- Ask questions
- Speak

• Respect others and the text
• Refer to the text

Assigned Seats

Don't underestimate the power of seating to affect the climate of a seminar. We usually start by asking students to choose their seats wisely, advising them not to sit next to people they think will make it difficult for them to participate successfully. However, students often do not choose wisely, so we turn to assigning seats.

What It Looks Like

• You know who among your students should not sit near each other, either because they will giggle and talk together or because they will poke and pinch and growl at each other. Spread them out.

• You also know who should sit right next to you so that you have a positive influence on them. This might be a disruptive student, a fidgety student, or a shy student.

• We use name cards in every seminar as a reminder to use names when talking to people, so one way we do seating charts is to have the name cards on the chairs when students enter the classroom. It's an easy way for students to know where to sit.

• We also tend to spread out the talkative people. We've noticed that students are more likely to speak if there are other people near them who are speaking.

Yellow Card, Red Card

Sometimes, it's very helpful for students to have a visual reminder of when they are acting inappropriately in a seminar. Also, a visual allows you to communicate with a student without interrupting the seminar. In our experience, students appreciate the visual warning and generally monitor their behavior well for the rest of the seminar to avoid being kicked out.

What It Looks Like

• Laminate a yellow sheet of paper and a red sheet of paper about the size of a 4×6-inch index card. Keep the cards in front of you while you facilitate.

• Before you begin, explain the system to students: as in soccer, you will "yellow card," or give a warning to anyone who is not adhering to seminar guidelines, especially regarding respect. A second violation will result in a "red card," which means the student can no longer participate. You should also tell students what the consequences are if they are dismissed from the seminar, which will depend on your classroom rules and your seminar objectives. Students should know in advance what task they must do if they are red carded so that you will not need to stop the seminar to instruct them. If possible, it is best to have the red-carded student physically withdraw from the seminar circle to re-establish a safe climate.

• During a seminar, if a student's behavior warrants a card, you will hold up the card, make eye contact with the student, and make a note on your map about the card.

Ejection

Generally, students who are involved in a seminar in a negative way really want to participate. Often, the best consequence is to take that privilege away until they're ready to participate safely. Whether or not you use a warning system, you must be ready and willing to remove students who are making the seminar unsafe if you want to achieve the safety necessary for a respectful intellectual exchange. The disruption such an ejection might cause during a seminar is well worth the benefit of the safety you will create when you return to the seminar.

What It Looks Like

What do you do with students when they're kicked out? As above, it's helpful if students know in advance what task they should do and where they should do it if they are excused from the seminar circle. Here are some ideas:

• If you have the room, you might have a designated seat outside the seminar circle with work for the student to do; preferably, the work is related to the seminar text and is not much fun.
• Tell the student to record the content of the seminar as accurately as possible.
• Tell the student to answer questions about the seminar text in writing.

- Have a designated observing task for the student to do (see Fishbowl in Chapter 7).
- Have the student reflect on why she or he was expelled from the seminar and what he or she will do differently next seminar.

Be sure to assess the student and hold him or her accountable for work done outside the seminar circle. Other consequences for ejection will depend on your classroom protocol.

Time-Out

Sometimes, the best way to de-escalate and diffuse an unsafe climate is simply to stop the seminar briefly.

What It Looks Like

- When gentle reminders don't work, call time-out. Tell students you are stepping out of the seminar for a minute.

- Reflect on how things are going: What is the group doing well? Ask them what they need to work on. Don't be afraid to be firm here as facilitator. It's your job to set parameters and enforce them so that the environment is safe. Let the climate settle down.

- Call time back in and resume the seminar.

- Allow plenty of time for debriefing and reflection at the end of the seminar.

Write Before You Talk

If you have students who are very talkative and don't self-monitor even after goal setting, you might need to slow down their talking, or even limit it.

What It Looks Like

- Before the seminar, tell students who tend to dominate the conversation to write their comments and questions down before they speak. Tell them you will check their papers after the seminar to see if they did it. Often, such students want to be sure to get their comment in before they forget, and writing helps eliminate this issue. Writing also forces the student to pause and think before speaking, and this allows others more talk time.

- Limit how many times those students talk. If students still dominate the seminar even after writing, you may need to tell them they can speak only a certain number of times in each seminar. This is an extreme measure, but it is sometimes necessary.

Role-Play

Sometimes students learn seminar skills better when simulating a seminar than when actually doing it. Through role-play, students can explore a wide range of seminar behaviors in small groups, as well as ways to improve negative behaviors.

What It Looks Like

• *General:* Divide the class into small groups, and ask each group to pick a seminar behavior that they think the class needs to work on. Ask them to illustrate the issue in a two-minute skit and then to illustrate a reversal or resolution of the issue in a follow-up two-minute skit. Give each group a few minutes to prepare, then let each group perform, allowing time for the other groups to guess the issue and offer comments and ideas after each skit.

• *Whole-class:* Give the class an issue to work on—for example, disagreeing respectfully or not interrupting—and spend a few minutes focusing only on that issue. This activity allows students to develop the specific skill you're working on.

• *Specific:* Give students index cards with specific roles described on one side; this can be done in small groups or as one large group. Roles might be Facilitator—trying to keep the conversation respectful, Interrupter—always interrupting, Talker—talks too much, Silent one—never talks, Arguer—always argues, Bored—not listening, Tired—not listening, Thinker, Side conversationalist, Pencil tapper, Rude commenter, and so on—whatever roles you want to highlight. Simulate a seminar for 5 to 10 minutes. Debrief after the seminar. Have students guess what each other's roles were. Then, have students flip their cards over. On the other side, the same things should be written on every card: "Wonderful seminar participant: listens, thinks, speaks when has an idea to contribute, asks questions, refers to text, treats everyone with respect." Simulate a seminar for another 5 to 10 minutes and then follow with a debriefing.

Stop and Try Again

If students can't handle the seminar format after all of the above interventions, stop the seminar and try again another day after more group and individual reflection.

SAFETY ISSUES: TIPTOEING

Building Safety Outside the Seminar

If your classroom is not a socially safe place on a regular basis, chances are that participating in a seminar will help, but will not magically transform your class. Besides typical issues of classroom management and establishing a climate for all to succeed, both of which are well beyond the scope of this book, you should look for opportunities to develop a collaborative, safe environment outside of the seminar.

What It Looks Like

• Getting-to-know-you activities—have students interview each other and introduce one another either verbally or in writing, for example.

• Initiatives/group problem-solving tasks, like the human knot (see, for example, http://www.wilderdom.com/games/descriptions/HumanKnot .html for a description of the human knot and http://www.wilderdom .com/games/InitiativeGames.html for descriptions of a variety of team-building activities).

• Cooperative learning—the more accustomed students are to working in pairs and small groups, the easier working with the large group in a seminar conversation will be.

Role-Play

Role-play can be particularly good for tiptoeing students because it frees them up from the more formal process of the seminar.

What It Looks Like

• Besides the role-play strategies described under Attacking Personalities, you can have students role-play disagreeing appropriately and challenging ideas in the text and discussion.

Have Seminars More Frequently

• Sometimes students tiptoe because the seminar format is unfamiliar to them or because they don't have enough practice to feel comfortable participating.

What It Looks Like

• Especially when students are just learning how to participate in seminars, we recommend having short seminars frequently rather than long seminars occasionally. In this stage of students' seminar participation development, your focus is on the seminar process. You want students to learn how the seminar works and how to participate well. You might have seminars for only 20 minutes initially: Students will learn the seminar process better through several 20-minute seminars than through one 60-minute seminar.

● How often should you do seminars? Initially, we recommend doing seminars once a week so that students (and facilitators!) get lots of practice in the process. Once students are more comfortable with the seminar format, you can shift to a frequency that aligns with your curriculum demands. In our experience, humanities (English and social studies) teachers tend to have seminars more frequently, once a week or once every other week; math and science teachers tend to have seminars every other week or every three weeks; and other disciplines, such as foreign language, physical education, technology, and art, tend to have seminars less frequently—once a month or once a quarter (they usually have less class time with students than the core academic disciplines). Whatever your discipline, you want to make sure that you and the students are getting enough practice with the seminar process that you can build on previous seminars, rather than starting over each time, re-learning how to safely participate.

Ask the Students

This strategy is so obvious that we often forget it in the classroom: Ask the students why they're tiptoeing. Often, the only way to tell why students are not fully participating is to ask them. In our experience, students are generally pretty honest, especially if they perceive that you sincerely want to hear what they have to say. Sometimes they need a little prompting, but they should be able to tell you whether the problem is with the text, their preparation, group dynamics, or some other reason you haven't thought of.

AUTHENTIC PARTICIPATION ISSUES: NONPARTICIPATION

Heads-Up Questions

Sometimes students are quiet because they like to have more time to think and process their ideas before speaking than the seminar allows.

What It Looks Like

● Before a seminar, tell your quiet students a question or questions you are planning to ask. Tell them you'd like to hear from them when you ask the question.

Pair-Share

Give students a chance to talk about an idea or question with a partner. Conversing with one person is less intimidating for most people than speaking with an entire group. Pair-sharing often helps generate lots of ideas and talk so that the conversational pump is well primed when you come back to the whole group.

What It Looks Like

• Before a seminar, ask students to discuss your opening question in pairs and then ask them to choose one person from their pair to share their thoughts with the group. This technique allows quieter students to speak in a more informal setting with a peer but does not require them to speak to the whole group. You can also give students other assignments to work on in pairs to prepare them for the seminar, such as defining unknown words or filling out a graphic organizer with information from the text.

• During a seminar, if there is more silence than even wait time can cure, try asking students to think about and discuss a particular question with their partner. You can get up and circulate among the pairs while students are speaking so that you have a sense of their conversations, can ask probing questions, and can troubleshoot why students are being quiet. When you feel you have allowed enough time for sharing, return to your seat and resume the whole-group seminar.

Round-Robin

Hearing quickly from every student, particularly early in a seminar, ensures that all students have spoken at least once and gets a range of ideas on the conversational table. Although we don't recommend that you start every seminar with a round-robin, it can be a highly effective jumping-off point.

What It Looks Like

• Ask an opening question that is something for which all participants should be able to generate a response. Examples: "What do you think the most important word (or line or detail, for art texts) is in this text? If you were going to title this text, what would your title be?" As you go around the circle, ask participants to give their answer but not to explain it yet. If students aren't ready when their turn comes, let them pass and tell them you'll return to them at the end of the circle. After all students have responded, tell students that the discussion is open for anyone who wants to share why they chose their particular answer.

- You can also use the round-robin during a seminar if you break into a pair-share and want to hear back from each pair. If you've done a pair-share earlier in the seminar, you can ask the partner who did not speak earlier to speak during this round-robin.

Inviting Quiet People to Speak

Although we recommend never calling on specific students to speak in a seminar, issuing a general invitation can open the floor for students who would like to speak but haven't been able to enter the conversation.

What It Looks Like

- If the seminar has been running for some time and several students have not spoken, try this: Before you ask a question, signal that the floor is open to quiet people by saying something like, "When I ask this question, we'd like to hear first from people who haven't spoken yet today." Then, be sure to allow wait time after you ask the question.

- If your students are like ours, invariably you will have a talkative student who just can't bear to wait for quiet people to talk and will ignore your request. Often, other students will correct the talkative student. If not, reiterating that you want to hear from people who *haven't* spoken, or trying the same line again with a different question usually works.

Reflective Writing

Sometimes allowing students to process their ideas in writing helps prepare them to speak.

What It Looks Like

- *Content:* During a seminar, ask all students to write their answer to a difficult question before resuming the discussion.

- *Process:* During a seminar, ask students to reflect on how they are participating. If it is a very quiet seminar and students are relying on you to ask all the questions and drive the conversation, this can be an opportunity for students to reflect on their mutual responsibility in the seminar—it's their conversation, and if no one speaks, it's not a very interesting conversation. This type of process reflection can also be helpful if you are taking a time-out for safety reasons. Rather than talk it out, let students write.

Follow-Up Writing

As we mentioned in the Assessment section in Chapter 7, post-seminar is a wonderful time to develop some of the ideas that went unspoken during the seminar and to help students bring the ideas from the text back to their own lives. If you give a writing assignment, you'll connect reading, speaking, and thinking to writing. Thus, the seminar becomes a pre-writing exercise for writing with depth of thought. Asking students to write also gives you the opportunity to respond with positive feedback that encourages quiet students to participate next time.

What It Looks Like

• For example, if you did a seminar on the Pledge of Allegiance, you might have students write their own pledge to something that is important to them. If you did a seminar on Martin Luther King Jr.'s "I Have a Dream" speech, you might ask students to write about whether they think King's dream has been realized or to write their own "I Have a Dream" speech.

• Often, we give students more than one option for post-seminar assignments—two different writing choices, as well as a drawing or acting option, depending on our objectives.

Positive Reinforcement

Sometimes the simplest strategies are the most effective. Although we do not advocate giving positive reinforcement during the seminar (we want students to own the conversation and not look to the facilitator to tell them whether they made a good comment), we do recommend giving positive feedback to students after the seminar. This is particularly true for quiet students. If quiet students make a comment during the seminar, tell them how glad you were to hear their contribution. If quiet students don't talk, tell them you could tell they were listening and you'd love to hear one of their thoughts next seminar. These little exchanges can go a long way toward getting students to add their voice to classroom seminars.

AUTHENTIC PARTICIPATION ISSUES: SUPERFICIAL PARTICIPATION

Some idea-hopping is natural, particularly at the beginning of a seminar and with nonprint texts, as participants toss ideas and digest the text. However, if the idea-hopping continues, you need to intervene to encourage participants to delve into topics more deeply.

Connections

Often, students' comments are disconnected from one another. For this strategy, focus students' attention on connecting their ideas to other ideas, rather than just interjecting a comment unrelated to anything else in the seminar.

What It Looks Like

• Focus your group goal-setting on building on each other's points.

• Ask students to identify how what they're saying relates to something someone else said. If you do this several times in a seminar, students will be annoyed, but they'll get the point and start making connections.

Question Again

Once you are past the initial exchanges in a seminar, if students are still idea-hopping, you may have to intervene frequently to keep them focused on a particular topic.

What It Looks Like

• Repeat the last question asked, and tell students to stay focused on that question.

• Rephrase the question. Perhaps students didn't understand it the way you asked it the first time.

• Take a recent student comment that seems worth pursuing and frame a follow-up question that pushes students to dig into the topic.

Pair-Share/Write During Seminar

Just as pair-sharing and writing can help quiet students gather their thoughts to speak, so to, can these strategies work to slow down the pace of the conversation so that talk can linger on one topic for a longer period of time.

What It Looks Like

• Give students a focused question to discuss with a partner. Students are often less anxious to get their idea out into the whole-group seminar after a pair-share because they've had a chance to tell the idea to someone already. When you return to the whole group, ask the question again, reminding students to connect their idea to someone else's.

• Give students a focused question to write about. Have them either share their answer with a partner before returning to the whole group or simply return to the whole group, again reminding students to connect their ideas.

Silence

If there is a lot of idea-hopping in the seminar, there probably is not a lot of silence. We're all conditioned to avoid silence in conversations, particularly in classrooms, where the teacher usually swoops in and breaks any silence with a question or comment. However, in the seminar, silence is a good thing (in moderation, of course. An entirely silent seminar is no fun at all.)

What It Looks Like

• Before the seminar, talk with students about how silence is good because it means people are thinking. Encourage them to allow silence in the seminar, perhaps counting to five before they speak.

• During the seminar, ask or re-ask a question, and tell students that you're going to give them some time to think before talking. Count to 10 (or whatever number feels excruciatingly long to you), and then invite them to respond to the question.

• On your seminar map, whenever there is a silence, count how long the silence is and mark it on your map. You'll be amazed how short the silences are compared to how long they feel.

• After a seminar, tell students about the silences: How many periods of silence exceeded three seconds? What was the longest period of silence? Ask them to debrief the silences: How do the silences feel to them? What's good (or bad) about silence? Students will start to notice silence more and will be more comfortable with it if you discuss it as a group.

Map Connections

Your seminar map can be a very useful tool for showing students whether they are idea-hopping or connecting ideas and delving into ideas.

What It Looks Like

• Map connections by drawing lines or arrows between students whenever a student connects to someone else's ideas. See Liz's map in Chapter 7 for an example of mapping lines. If students are idea-hopping, there will be very few lines on the map. If students are digging into the text and building on ideas, the map will be messy, with many lines.

• Show students your map of the seminar. Remember that mapping on an overhead transparency makes it easier to show the whole class the map at the same time. This visual representation of how well they are connecting ideas sometimes helps students focus on building on each other's points. Students like to see the map, the visual record of their progress as they get better at connecting ideas in future seminars. If you save maps in your seminar folder, you can compare maps to look for progress.

• On your map, you can also tally how many times students talk about a certain topic or how long they talk about a topic before switching to a new one. Share this information with students during the debriefing.

CHALLENGE ISSUES: POPCORN

Where in the Text?

One of the best strategies we've found for slowing students down when they pop from one idea to the next is to ask them to support their statement with evidence from the text.

What It Looks Like

• Every time students make a comment, ask them, "Where do you see support for that in the text?" Students will roll their eyes and complain, but if you consistently ask them to point to the place in the text that supports their comments, they'll catch on pretty quickly and will start citing the text automatically. Asking students "where in the text" serves several purposes: It slows them down, requiring them to spend more time on one idea; it keeps them on the text and makes it obvious when they stray away from the text (because they can't find text support for their comment); and it teaches them the discipline and skill of finding text-based evidence to support their ideas.

Ask Follow-Up Questions

Another way to encourage students to pursue a particular topic or idea in more depth is to ask follow-up questions.

What It Looks Like

• Follow up with the particular student by asking that student questions about his or her idea. For example: "Why do you say that? What do you mean by _____? Could you explain a little bit more about _____? Where in the text do you see support for that idea?"

• Follow up with all the students in the seminar circle by addressing the follow-up questions to the group as a whole rather than to a particular student. For example: "How do you think the text does or does not support Dominique's idea that _____? How do you think Marie's idea relates to the idea that Jeremy offered earlier in the seminar, that [paraphrase Jeremy's idea]?"

Paraphrase and Probe

Generally, to let the seminar really be the students' conversation, we prefer to let students speak for themselves without having their words filtered by us as the facilitators. However, sometimes paraphrase can be an effective participation tool, particularly when you want to guide students to delve more deeply into a particular topic.

What It Looks Like

• If several students are circling around a similar idea, paraphrase the overall idea and then ask follow-up questions related to the idea. Possible questions include: "What do you think the author would say in response to that idea, based on the text? How does this idea connect to the idea you were discussing earlier about _____? Let's stay on this idea of _____ for a little while. What other ideas do people have about it?" (This is a good place to invite people who haven't spoken yet into the conversation.)

• Surface the general idea by putting a name to it. Then, ask specific questions about it. For example, "I'm hearing lots of conversation that seems to be related to the idea of equality. How do you think the author would define equality based on the text?" or "Where in the text does the author seem to be talking about equality?" or "How do you think the notion of equality fits with the discussion you were having earlier in the seminar about freedom?"

Pair-Share/Write During the Seminar

The same strategies you've used for slowing students down and allowing them time and structure to be more thoughtful work here, too.

What It Looks Like

• Paraphrase or summarize what students have been talking about. Give students a question or two that helps them dig into the idea in more depth. Ask them to respond to the question by talking with a partner or by writing. Then, either pose the question to the whole group, or do a round-robin by asking each pair to share a response before opening the conversation back up to the whole group.

CHALLENGE ISSUES: ROSETTA STONE

Pre-Seminar

Make sure students are prepared to talk about the content of the text. Sometimes students don't participate because they don't have enough background context or comprehension of the text to offer insight into the text.

What It Looks Like

The type of preparation you do will depend greatly on the text and on students, but here are a few general suggestions:

- *Defining unknown vocabulary words.* Students can do this for homework or as class work before a seminar. More informally, you can ask before the seminar if there are any words for which participants aren't sure about the definition. Then, have other students define them orally, or offer your own definitions.

- *Annotating.* Teach students how to annotate or mark up a text. This may involve your modeling on an overhead how to underline, write comments, ask questions, circle unfamiliar words, and so on. We have found it easier to teach some students how to interact with a text using nonprint texts. We laminate copies of the text, such as an art print, and then give students wet-erase markers to mark up the text. They enjoy it and can then transfer the skill to print texts with guidance. The laminated texts can be cleaned and reused with the next class.

- *Guided reading.* Give students guidance about what they should be looking for as they read. You might have comprehension questions. Or, you might ask them to summarize the content of the text, or chunk it into smaller pieces. Again, this can be homework or class work, and it is important for texts that will be difficult for students. With particularly challenging texts, you may want to work through the comprehension of the piece together with students.

- *Graphic organizers.* Use a variety of graphic organizers as part of helping students comprehend and interact with the text. If students are reading Langston Hughes's story, "Thank You, Ma'am," they might make a list of characteristics of each of the two leading characters. Then, in your opening question for the seminar, you could ask them to choose one word to describe each character. You could use Venn diagrams, compare/contrast charts—all the graphic organizer tools you normally use in your classroom.

- *Read aloud.* Read the text aloud, especially with texts that were meant to be read aloud, such as poems and speeches. Ask for one or two volunteers to read the text aloud before the seminar. This is also a good technique for any type of shorter text, as participants often hear something they may not have picked up when they read.

- *Pair-share.* Ask students to talk with a partner before the seminar. They could complete a graphic organizer together; they could consider the opening question together; they could answer a different question you pose to prepare them.

- *Context.* Be sure to give participants any background knowledge they need in order to be able to discuss the text well. This might be information about the author, about the historical time period of the text, about the audience for or purpose of the text, for example. With some texts, little or no background is necessary; with other texts, you may want to study a topic for weeks before doing a seminar related to the topic.

- *Admission ticket.* If you have issues with students not reading and preparing to discuss the text before a seminar, use students' written preparation as an admission ticket to the seminar—if they have it, they can participate; if not, they sit outside the seminar circle and observe seminar behaviors.

A Different Type of Text

Try to discern why students aren't talking. If the classroom is safe, perhaps the issue is the text itself. Is the text too narrow and obvious? Is it too challenging or not challenging enough? Is it relevant enough to the curriculum? Do students have enough context? Perhaps you should choose a different text.

What It Looks Like

- The Seminar Text Rubric (see Chapter 1) is a tool for gauging how appropriate a text is for the seminar format. Texts that fall in the 2's and 3's on the rubric are good candidates for a seminar. However, if a text is 3 on challenging, students may need extra support both before and during the seminar for entering and understanding the text. Anything that scores a 1 on the ambiguity category is probably not a very challenging or rich text, and students probably will have little to say about it. Likewise, a text that scores a 1 on curricular relevance may seem out of context for students, and they may have little to say about it, even if it is otherwise a great text.

- Try a nonprint text. If students have not been participating with a print text, a nonprint text may feel more accessible to them. Nonprint texts with a lot of visual detail often provide a good entry point for students to discuss complex ideas and to learn how to notice details in a text.

- Vary types of text in general. Our students weary of looking at the same sorts of texts over time, so we tend to look for different types of text. The only real requirement is that it be something tangible (e.g., not an idea or value, like "war and peace," but a text that addresses war and peace). We've used maps, poems, historical documents, paintings, essays, short stories, math problems, photographs, sculpture, monuments, charts (like the periodic table), and myths, just to name a few types of text.

- Remember that a text may seem full of ambiguity, curricular relevance, big ideas, and challenge, and students still may not engage with it. This may simply be a matter of the particular ebb and flow of young people, but it may also be developmental in the seminar sense. Generally, when students are first learning how to participate in a seminar, it's wise to choose shorter texts, a range of types of text (including nonprint), and texts that aren't too difficult to read. The texts should have complex ideas, but it's better if the language is not too complex. You want participants to focus first on developing the social skills involved in seminar participation and then later to focus on developing the intellectual skills necessary to engage with difficult texts.

Good Questions

Sometimes the conversation doesn't go anywhere because neither the facilitator nor the students are asking good questions. In a seminar, "good" questions are open ended, clear, thought provoking, and grounded in the text. (See Chapter 1 for a more in-depth explanation of question writing.)

What It Looks Like

- Before a seminar, plan questions that you will ask during the different parts (opening, middle, and closing). We never ask quite the same questions that we plan in advance, but planning them helps us listen to the conversation to see whether we should ask a question we planned or create a new question based on the conversation. Planning ahead also lets us examine the questions to see whether they are open ended, clear, thought provoking, and grounded in the text.

- Before a seminar, ask a colleague to look at your planned questions to see whether he or she thinks they are open ended, clear, 'thought provoking, and grounded in the text, and whether he or she has any other ideas for questions. Better yet, write the questions while working with at least one other colleague. Questions almost always come out better when at least two minds work on them together.

- During the seminar, if you get little or no response to a question you asked, rephrase the question to make it clearer for students. Despite our best efforts to design clear questions before we start a seminar, inevitably a question doesn't seem nearly as clear to students as it seemed to us when preparing. We usually try to say it another way and see if that works any better.

- Sometimes either the facilitator or a participant will ask a question that the group isn't quite ready to answer. This most frequently happens early in a seminar when participants haven't had enough time to wrestle with the text but are faced with a challenging question. If after wait time students haven't engaged with the question, we usually say that we'll hold that question and return to it later in the seminar. We make a note of the question on our seminar map so that we remember to return to it later, particularly if it's a student's question, as opposed to our own question. We then offer a different question to restart and redirect the conversation.

OWNERSHIP ISSUES: DICTATORSHIP

Relinquish the Reins

For some facilitators, this is the most difficult strategy, but it can also be the most rewarding. Remember, the ideal you're aiming for is that students drive the conversation with you there to accelerate, brake, and gently steer the conversation to help them get to a deeper understanding of the text, themselves, and each other. Try turning over some of the responsibility for the direction and content of the conversation to the students rather than controlling it all yourself.

What It Looks Like

- Even though you should always have a seminar plan before you begin a seminar, you should also always expect that plan to change depending on what students say. We don't think we've ever had a seminar in which we've asked exactly the questions we had planned. The plan is a guideline, but you should be open to changing direction, asking different questions, and engaging a different component of the text than you had originally envisioned. As long as students are staying with the text—in other words, they can support their ideas with evidence from the text—you should try to take what they're seeing in the text and help them go deeper with their ideas rather than enforcing your own agenda.

- Remind students at the beginning of a seminar that they can ask questions, too. You might set a group goal of students asking a few questions so that they begin to rely less on you for questions to drive the conversation.

- We've seen some facilitators ask participants to generate questions before the seminar and then use some of those questions during the seminar.

- You know that students are beginning to drive the seminar on their own when the conversation doesn't depend on you. So, for example, if the pattern of interaction in a seminar is that you ask a question, a few students answer, and then everyone waits for you to ask another question, then you are driving the conversation. If, however, the pattern of interaction in a seminar is that someone asks a question (you or a student) or makes a comment, several students respond, and then a student asks a different question or takes the conversation to another idea with a comment, then students are driving the conversation. Focus on who is responsible for changes in direction and for new ideas. As a facilitator, sometimes you will take the lead because that's part of your job, but ideally, students will also sometimes initiate shifts and introduce ideas.

Self-Assessment

Several different strategies for self-assessment will help you get a picture of how much you are controlling the conversation.

What It Looks Like

- *Ask yourself questions.* Ideally, take five minutes within 24 hours of your seminar, and write answers to your questions. That way, you'll have a record of your responses, and you can look for changes over time. Some questions you might want to consider are: How many of the questions you planned did you ask? Did you ask them in the order you anticipated? How many unplanned questions did you ask? What new things did you learn from the conversation? What unexpected directions did the seminar go in? What points did students bring up that were ignored in the conversation? Who talked the most in the seminar? Were students talking to each other or to you?

• *Map the seminar.* Look for patterns of interaction. Did students connect ideas with one another, or did they participate in solo "this is what I think" fashion? Who asked the questions in the seminar? Are students participating fairly evenly, or are just a few students dominating the conversation? (You might not be the only oppressor in the seminar circle . . .) How many times did you talk and for how long?

• *Watch a videotape* of a seminar and focus on your role as facilitator. You might answer the above questions as you watch the video. In addition, you could look at what the purpose of your questions is—Are you filling silence? Are you pushing a particular idea deeper? Are you changing direction?

• *Have others watch you.* Peer colleagues and students can serve both as observers and as feedback providers. Students usually love the role of watching you and letting you know what they saw. Most observers are more helpful to you when you give them some direction about what you want them to look for—for example, count how many times you talk, write down all the questions you ask, tell you whether you're talking too much, not enough, or just right.

• *Ask the students.* Before the seminar, tell them you're setting a personal goal of not dominating the conversation and are trying to support them having the conversation. After the seminar, ask them for feedback on how you did meeting your goal and share your own reflections with them. This technique will both model seminar behavior for students and make explicit your vision of participation for both you and them.

Wait Time

This strategy serves a number of different purposes, but it's key for avoiding dictatorship. Silences in a seminar can be positively nerve wracking for participants and facilitators. We're not used to silence in classrooms. Based on previous schooling, students will expect the facilitator to interrupt the silence with a question or comment. However, in a seminar, you must fight the urge to speak during silent periods.

What It Looks Like

• One of the best signals you can give students that a seminar is not the typical classroom activity is by waiting a long time before you speak. Give students time to wrestle with the text. Don't jump in with another question. Count to 30 and doodle on your paper while you wait.

• Tell students before the seminar that you will allow silences and that you will not rescue them if it is quiet. This helps signal to students that if they want rescuing from the silence, they're going to have to do it themselves. If students are willing to take ownership of the seminar and are waiting for there to be space in the conversation unfilled by you, they will say something during the silence and steer the conversation.

Favorite-Text Phenomenon

Be cautious when using a text that you love or that you know so well that you might not be able to hear other opinions about it. We're guilty of doing this ourselves many a time. Occasionally, it turns out OK, but more often than not, we're disappointed in the seminar and not as open to what direction students want to take the conversation.

What It Looks Like

• Be wary of picking a text that is a favorite of yours—we all have a tendency to push students to like the text, too, and to see it the way we see it. The point of a seminar is not that students like or admire the text; it is that they engage in thoughtful dialogue with each other about the ideas in the text.

• Don't use a text that you think you know everything about already. It will be hard for you to hear new ideas and help the conversation build around them, rather than your own ideas.

• Don't use a text that you think can be interpreted in only one "right" way. You will inevitably ask not-so-open questions in which you try to guide students toward a particular way of seeing the text.

• We hope that you are excited about the texts you use and that you introduce students to some of your favorite writers and artists and thinkers through a seminar. However, the question to ask yourself is whether you're OK with students offering an interpretation different from your own. If you can't say yes, choose a different text.

Eye Contact

Eye contact tells you a lot about who is in control of the seminar. If you're looking at students or students are looking at you, then you're still at the center of the seminar. If students are looking at each other instead of you, then students are at the center of the seminar.

What It Looks Like

• Try not to make eye contact with students. Look down at your map. Before a seminar, tell students why you won't be making eye contact with them. You're not being rude; you just want it to be their conversation, so you're going to help it be their conversation by not looking at them. Students will quite naturally look at you for validation when they are learning how to participate in the seminar. And you will quite naturally look at them to give validation and to listen when you are learning how to participate in the seminar. However, avoiding eye contact sends a powerful signal that you are a backseat driver in the seminar.

● Encourage students to make eye contact with each other. The group might set this as a group goal in the pre-seminar period and debrief how they did with the goal post-seminar.

OWNERSHIP ISSUES: ANARCHY

Many of the tips under safety work here. Here are some other ideas.

Don't Be Afraid—Drive

Being the facilitator does not mean you have completely turned over control of the seminar to students. You are the facilitator, so it is your responsibility to take control of the conversation when (or before!) chaos erupts.

What It Looks Like

● Ask a question to steer the conversation in a particular direction.

● Call a time-out to get the seminar back under control.

● Restate some of what has been said, and follow up with a question to help focus the conversation.

● Read a quote or point out a detail from the text, and ask a question about the quote/detail to help bring back conversations that have strayed far from the text.

Turn-Taking

If students aren't listening to each other at all and keep interrupting, try a turn-taking strategy. Eventually, you do not want students to rely on turn-taking because you want them to learn how to have a respectful, free-flowing conversation with each other. Sometimes, however, they need to experience formal turn-taking to learn how to self-monitor who talks when.

What It Looks Like

- "Three before me": tell students that at least three different people need to speak before they can speak again. This will also help avoid back-and-forth debates between two people to the exclusion of the rest of the group.

- Tell students they can speak only a certain number of times in a single seminar. We tend to use this strategy only with individual talkative students, but we have seen some people use it with entire groups.

- Pass a soft object. Only the person holding the object is allowed to speak. This serves as a visual signal for whose turn it is to speak. The danger is that students get more interested in passing/throwing/having the object than they do in contributing meaningfully to the seminar. However, it can be a useful strategy for teaching students how to take turns.

Look Around the Circle

Yes, we know we told you not to make eye contact, but it is worth making the occasional visual scan of the seminar landscape.

What It Looks Like

- We tend to do these visual scans while we offer questions to the group. We try to look around the circle so that participants know the question is directed toward everyone.

- We also sneak a look when participants are talking with each other. We avoid looking at participants directly after we ask a question, and we don't make eye contact with any particular student when we raise our heads just enough to check in for the things we can't hear. We check to see: Who looks like they're not listening or participating? How many students look engaged in the conversation? Who is looking at the text? Who looks confused? What does the body language in the room say?

- And occasionally, we use eye contact intentionally to signal to individual students that their behavior is inappropriate. Because students are used to no eye contact from the facilitator, they understand that eye contact with a mimed or telepathic message means that they are out of bounds on seminar decorum, and they usually improve their behavior—at least for a few minutes.

Resource A

Training Guides

USING THE FULCRUMS FOR PROFESSIONAL DEVELOPMENT

This book was written to address a particular need in understanding seminar facilitation. As we mentioned in the first chapter, the Socratic/Paideia seminar has a strong history as an instructional tool, and a number of published resources address the basic skills of seminar facilitation.

In this book, we have provided an overview of seminar instruction and an introduction to our model of seminar facilitator decision making. Resource A describes ways to use this book as a tool for teacher professional development. We outline ways staff developers can use the fulcrums and decision-making model to help new and experienced seminar facilitators become more successful with their students. We also describe a variety of ways for individuals and groups of teachers to use this book. We hope that staff developers will be able to use Resource A to plan training sessions and that individual teachers will use it to help them develop further as seminar facilitators.

WORKING WITH GROUPS OF TEACHERS

New Facilitators

New facilitators need to focus primarily on getting the basics of seminar down—choosing texts, writing questions, and planning pre- and post-seminar activities. In our experience, some new facilitators find the fulcrum framework helpful, and others find it overwhelming as they try to manage all the components of seminar. Therefore, at the most, we recommend providing an initial brief introduction to the fulcrums and decision-making model, with an emphasis on the importance of safety and a developmental approach to seminar (both with students and facilitators).

All facilitators should keep a seminar folder—it's a good habit for new facilitators to get into from the beginning. The seminar folder should include:

- Seminar plan (which includes a space for post-seminar reflection notes)
- Text
- Basic Seminar Checklist
- Map (new facilitators may not map much initially, which is fine, but they should put any notes they make during a seminar in their folder)
- Fulcrum-Based Seminar Rubric
- Facilitator Reflection Form

After facilitators lead their first seminar, they should use both the Basic Seminar Checklist and Fulcrum-Based Seminar Rubric to assess the experience. Teachers should plan their next seminar using the Seminar Planning Form and Facilitator Reflection Form. Reproducible versions of these can be found in Resource B.

After one or two more seminars, there should be a more intensive training session using the decision-making model (see below for ideas about what this might look like). During this session, strategies for balancing the fulcrums should be discussed, using examples from the teachers' first few seminars. Teachers should bring with them their seminar maps, fulcrum rubrics, and any other artifacts from their seminar facilitation.

As teachers become more experienced with facilitation, they should engage in some of the professional development opportunities discussed in the rest of Resource A to continue developing their facilitation skills.

Experienced Facilitators

In the sample professional development session (or sessions, depending on available time) that follows, the person leading the session serves as the seminar facilitator. This session introduces the fulcrum framework to experienced facilitators:

- Begin with a whole-group seminar. Enough time must be devoted to the seminar for participants to experience an authentic, although perhaps abbreviated, seminar cycle.

- Briefly introduce the fulcrums.
- Hand out the Fulcrum-Based Seminar Rubric, and give participants an opportunity to assess the seminar and discuss it in small groups.
- Share analyses. Facilitator discusses his or her decision making using the fulcrums. Use blank flowchart overhead to explain decision making.
- Share the decision-making model, using the flowchart from Chapter 6.
- Have participants write about a specific moment during a seminar when they thought one of the fulcrums was out of balance. (Ideally, you have asked them to do this before the session). Participants share their stories with a partner. They then discuss what they think the issue was at that particular moment and which fulcrum was out of balance. With their partner, participants can complete a blank flowchart describing their decision-making process.
- Whole-group discussion of seminar moments and decision-making process.
- Assignment for the next professional development session: Write a case study of a moment when one of the fulcrums was in balance. What were you doing? Write another case study of a moment when one of the fulcrums was out of balance. What did you attempt as a strategy to balance the fulcrum?

Ideas for Follow-Up Sessions

- *Case-study protocol:* Participants share case studies in groups of three. One person shares his or her case study (either of a moment when the fulcrums were out of balance or when they were in balance) [3 minutes]. The other participants ask any clarifying questions they need answers to in order to be able to think about the case [2 minutes]. Then, the participants discuss which fulcrums they think were in or out of balance and discuss the decisions the facilitator should consider, as well as possible strategies the facilitator could try [5 minutes]. Finally, the person sharing the case study responds to what he or she has heard and describes what he or she will try in the next seminar [3 minutes]. Continue with the other participants sharing their case studies one at a time. This process can be used either to look at fulcrums in balance or at fulcrums out of balance. In either case, after each person in the triads has shared their case study, the triads should take a couple of minutes to brainstorm challenges, decisions, or strategies they shared. The whole group should then debrief, making a list of common challenges, decisions, and strategies.

- *Strategies:* Participants brainstorm key challenges they are facing in their seminars. Together, they brainstorm possible strategies to address these challenges. Then, they turn to Chapter 8 of this book for other ideas based on which fulcrum poses the greatest challenge. Each participant notes at least one new strategy to try in his or her next seminar.

- *Observations:* Participants should choose a partner whom they can observe once between professional development sessions. The observer should either focus specifically on a fulcrum or issue designated by the facilitator or should take general observation notes during the seminar. When the partners debrief after the seminar, they can use the fulcrum-based Rubric for Seminar Decision Making to identify areas of balance and areas not in balance. They should also discuss the facilitator's decisions and strategies used during the seminar, as well as any ideas for how to balance fulcrums in the future.

- *Variation:* Videotape a seminar, and show segments of the videotape in a whole-group session. Proceed as detailed in the previous Observations strategy.

- *Modeling:* An experienced facilitator does a demonstration seminar in another teacher's class. This strategy is especially effective when facilitators are just learning the process of seminar, but it can also be effective for modeling a specific issue, such as how to relinquish strict teacher control in the seminar or how to ask probing questions. Ideally, several teachers will observe the seminar. Alternatively, the session can be videotaped for teachers who are not able to attend. The facilitator and the teacher-observers debrief after the seminar, noting which fulcrums were in and out of balance and what the facilitator was doing that affected the fulcrums.

- *Variation:* A teacher demonstrates in his or her own classroom with other teachers observing, around an issue the group has identified that they want to address.

- *Envisioning:* Participants generate statements describing each fulcrum when balanced. What does it look like? What does it sound like? What are the students doing? What type of language are they using? How are they relating to the text? What are students not doing? What is the facilitator doing? What isn't the facilitator doing? Sometimes envisioning a balanced seminar can help in thinking about what strategies you would need to use to get your own seminar in balance.

- *Seminar Planning and Reflection Session:* Facilitators bring their seminar folders to a professional development session. They share one of their seminar plans, including the seminar map and reflection, and comment on their decision-making process. Facilitators work in pairs or small teams to design a seminar plan for a new text, focusing on how they might address any fulcrum issues they are having.

- Ideally, most follow-up professional development will be a combination of working with facilitators in their classrooms based on their actual seminars and working with the whole group together to identify common challenges and strategies.

WORKING ON YOUR OWN/WORKING WITH INDIVIDUAL TEACHERS

Individual Teachers

We know that some readers of this book are individual teachers interested in becoming more successful seminar facilitators. Some of you may work in a school in which no other teachers are using seminars or at least that has no school or districtwide staff development effort. These strategies can also be used by staff developers working with individual teachers.

The key elements for developing seminar facilitation on your own are:

- Enlisting students' help
- Self-assessing your seminar performance using the Fulcrum-Based Seminar Rubric
- Identifying specific fulcrum moments
- Focusing your facilitation based on the assessment of prior seminars.

Before you focus on the decisions you make during seminar, you need to make sure you have addressed the basics of seminars. The decisions you make outside of a seminar will have an impact on the seminar, so don't ignore the things you do to prepare for the seminar. If you have not addressed the basic elements of a seminar, you should focus on those first and then consider applying the fulcrum model. The Basic Seminar Checklist (see Chapter 1) will help you make sure you address the fundamentals of the seminar process.

Having Your Students Help in Seminar Development

Enlisting students' help accomplishes three things: (1) it increases students' awareness of what a seminar should look and feel like, (2) provides language for discussing seminar development and analysis, and (3) provides feedback for you. Show students the Fulcrum-Based Seminar Rubric, describe the fulcrums, and use the rubric when debriefing after the seminar. Students are usually honest about what's working and not working in a seminar. You can also videotape a seminar and have students watch all or parts of it, using the fulcrum-based rubric.

Self-Assessing Seminar Using the Fulcrum-Based Seminar Rubric

Alternatively, or perhaps in addition, you can self-assess your seminar performance using the Fulcrum-Based Seminar Rubric. You may want to videotape or audiotape a seminar to help you because you will notice more when you are simply watching or listening and not trying to facilitate. You can combine this strategy with the next strategy.

Identifying Specific Fulcrum Moments

Sometimes it is helpful to focus on a specific moment of a seminar in addition to looking at the whole seminar. The Fulcrum-Based Seminar Plan and Reflection Form can help in this process (see Resource B).

Focusing Your Facilitation Based on the Assessment of Prior Seminars

Based on your assessments of previous seminars, choose a facilitation focus for your next seminar. Choose a specific fulcrum that you think that you and your students need to work on and prepare to use a few strategies that will help you to balance this fulcrum (see Part III of this book for ideas of strategies). Set goals for your seminars based on this fulcrum focus. Keeping a seminar folder can help with the process of building on your prior facilitation. See above for a description of the seminar folder.

Study Group/Peer Coaching

Although we believe that an individual teacher will find this book and the tools within it helpful in becoming a more successful seminar facilitator, we also believe that the learning will be more effective if the teacher has the opportunity to work with colleagues interested in improving their seminar facilitation skills. There is a variety of effective ways to develop new skills collaboratively, most of which can be classified as either study groups or peer coaching. We encourage individual teachers to seek out colleagues and apply the professional development strategies described earlier in Resource A.

Resource B

Reproducibles

Basic Seminar Checklist

☐ The text chosen is appropriate for a seminar (see seminar rubric) and the development of the students.

☐ Prepared questions are open-ended (not leading) and designed to elicit higher-order thinking about the ideas in the text.

☐ The seminar plan includes pre- and post-seminar activities (see Seminar Planning Form).

☐ Students have all read the text and established a basic comprehension.

☐ The room is set up to allow all participants to make eye contact with each other (e.g., circle or square).

Seminar Planning Form

Text: _____ Class: _____

Pre-Seminar

Content—Present relevant background information. Prepare participants to discuss selected text.

Process—Review seminar objectives and guidelines. Prepare participants to participate in seminar discussion, and set goal[s].

Seminar Questions

Opening—Identify main ideas from the text.

Core—Focus/analyze textual details.

Closing—Personalize and apply the textual ideas.

Post-Seminar

Process—Assess individual and group participation, with students referring to recent past as well as future seminar discussion.

Content—Extend application of textual and discussion ideas; continuation of pre-seminar.

Facilitator Reflection Form

Reflect on the discussion and make a short statement about each fulcrum (for your primary fulcrum focus, you may want a more detailed description). You should consult your seminar map, notes, and any assessments (e.g., Fulcrum-Based Seminar Rubric) associated with the seminar.

Safety *is in balance when many students are participating and there are no side conversations, sarcasm, or teasing. How was safety today?*

Authentic Participation *is in balance when student comments refer directly to the text or to another participant's comments and are made in a respectful manner. How was authentic participation today?*

Challenge *is in balance when student comments address the complexities of the text's ideas and deepen understanding. How was challenge today?*

Ownership *is in balance when discussion is lively and focused on understanding ideas in the text; students are asking most of the critical questions. How was ownership today?*

Identify a moment in the seminar in which you felt a fulcrum was either out of balance or in balance. Briefly describe this moment. Be sure to include enough detail to help you remember the moment when you read this in the future.

If you chose an out-of-balance moment, which strategies did you try or would you like to try in the future? If you chose an in-balance moment, what were you doing in seminar that contributed most to the balance?

What modifications would you make to this plan for future seminars (pre-seminar, questions, etc.)?

Fulcrum-Based Seminar Rubric

5	4	3	2	1	Balanced	1	2	3	4	5

Attacking personalities
Many participants are attacking other participants. Participants laugh at the comments of others and/or make sarcastic comments. — **Some**

Few — Balanced — **Few**

Tiptoeing
Some Many participants are not challenging the ideas from the text or from other participants.

SAFETY

Many students are participating and offering a variety of ideas about the text.
Comments are related to the text. There are no side conversations, sarcasm, or teasing.

Comments:

5	4	3	2	1	Balanced	1	2	3	4	5

Non-Participation

Many participants are not focused on the discussion or text. **Few** participants are joining the discussion. Little or no interaction among participants when ideas are shared.

Some

Few

AUTHENTIC PARTICIPATION

Students are making comments that relate directly to the text or to another participant's comments; done in respectful manner.

Few

Some

Superficial participation

Many comments are not related closely to the text or discussion. Attention-seeking participation evident, and unsupported and/or rambling comments made.

Comments:

5	4	3	2	1	Balanced	1	2	3	4	5

Popcorn

Many unsupported comments or superficial lines of thinking. Ideas left undeveloped or challenged. — **Some** ... **Few**

CHALLENGE

Student comments address the complexities of the ideas in the text and continue to deepen understanding.

Few ... **Some Many**

Rosetta Stone

comments seem to be guesses or Òstabs-in-the-dark.Ó Active discussion, but ideas are being repeated and not developed.

Comments:

5	4	3	2	1	Balanced	1	2	3	4	5

Dictator
Facilitator is asking **most** of the questions and few participant lines of thinking are allowed to develop. The conversation is being directed through and by the facilitator.

Some

Few

Few

Some   Discussion is lively and focused on ideas in the text; however, **many** opportunities for probing particular ideas or connecting previously shared ideas are missed.

Anarchy

OWNERSHIP

Discussion is lively and focused on developing and understanding ideas in the text. Students are asking most of the critical questions.

Comments:

Safety is balanced when many students are participating
and there are no side conversations, sarcasm, or teasing.

Attacking Personalities

Tiptoeing

Indicators:

- Hurt students
- Non-participation
- Future reluctance to participate

Indicators:

- Few ideas challenged
- Intellectually weak seminar
- Stale environment

Safety

Authentic Participation is balanced when student comments refer directly to the text or to another participant's comments and are made in a respectful manner.

Non-Participation

Indicators:
- Silent students
- Unfocused students
- Little interaction among participants

Superficial Participation

Indicators:
- Mere talking
- Unsupportable statements
- Expert-parroting

Authentic Participation

Challenge is balanced when student comments address the
complexities of the ideas in the text and deepen understanding.

Popcorn

Results:
- Off-topic conversations
- Unsupportable lines
  of thinking
- Idea-hopping

Challenge

Rosetta stone

Results:
- Little or no participation
- "Stabs-in-the-dark"
- Circular conversation

Owenership is balanced when discussion is lively and focused on understanding ideas in the text. Students are asking most of the critical questions.

Dictatorship

Indicators:

- Frustrated students
- Facilitator-centered conversation
- Intellectually weak seminar

Anarchy

Indicators:

- Undisciplined argumentation
- Riotous and indignant debates
- Students left out of conversation

Ownership

Seminar Decision Making

1. Identify the issue.

2. Identify possible causes of the issue.

3. Match the cause to a particular fulcrum.

4. Identify and apply possible strategies to address the cause.

5. Assess the effectiveness of the strategy and determine next steps.

Seminar Facilitation Decision-Making Model

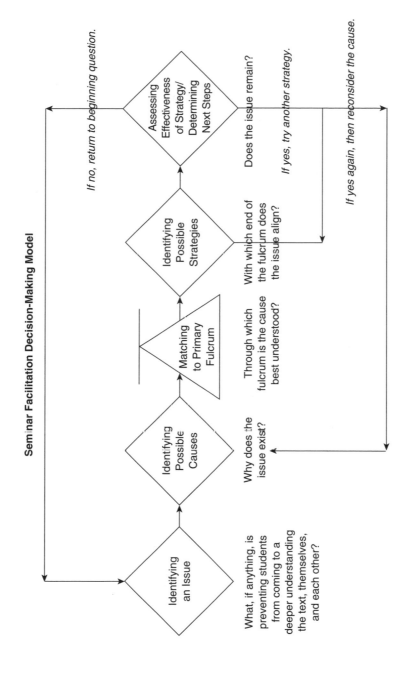

Seminar Facilitation Decision-Making Model

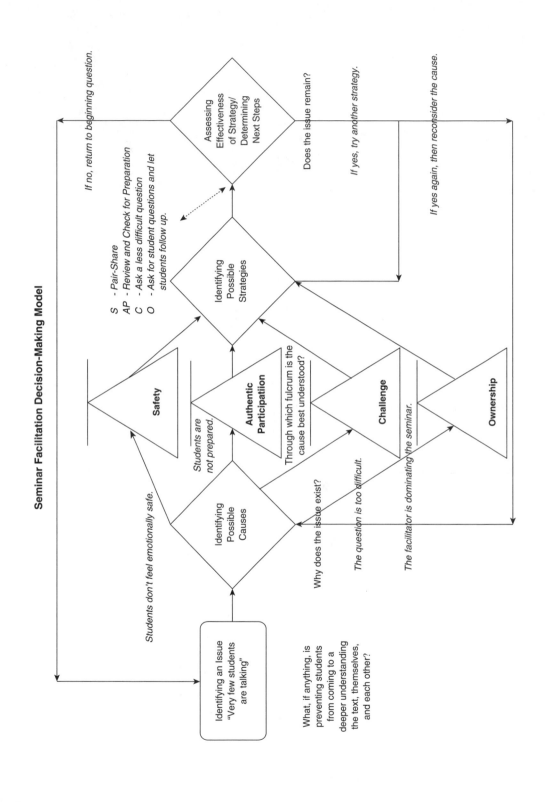

Strategies for Improving Discussions

Strategies	Page #	Safety	Authentic Participation	Challenge	Ownership
Reflection		▓	▓	▓	▓
Seminar mapping		▓	▓	▓	▓
Teaching the fulcrums to students		▓	▓	▓	▓
Fishbowl		▓	▓	▓	▓
Seminar folders		▓	▓	▓	▓
Videotape		▓	▓	▓	▓
Assessment		▓	▓	▓	▓
Peer planning		▓	▓	▓	▓
Peer coaching		▓	▓	▓	▓
Case study		▓	▓	▓	▓
Seminar ground rules		▓			
Assigned seats		▓			
Yellow card, red card		▓			
Ejection					
Time-out		▓			▓
Write before you talk		▓	▓		
Role-play		▓			
Stop		▓			
Building safety outside seminar		▓			
Have seminars more frequently					
Ask the students			▓		
Heads-up questions			▓		
Pair-share			▓	▓	
Round-robin		▓	▓		
Inviting quiet people to speak		▓	▓		
Reflective writing			▓	▓	
Follow-up writing			▓		
Positive reinforcement		▓	▓		
Connections			▓		
Question again			▓	▓	
Silence			▓	▓	▓
Map connections			▓	▓	
Where in the text?				▓	
Ask follow-up questions				▓	
Paraphrase and probe					
Pre-seminar					
Choosing a different text					
Good questions			▓		
Relinquish the reins					▓
Self-assessment					▓
Wait time			▓		▓
Favorite-text phenomenon					▓
Eye contact			▓		▓
Don't be afraid—drive		▓			▓
Turn-taking		▓			▓
Look around the circle		▓	▓		▓
Have fun		▓	▓	▓	▓

Note: Gray tones indicate which strategies can be applied to a particular fulcrum.

Index

CORWIN PRESS

The Corwin Press logo—a raven striding across an open book—represents the union of courage and learning. Corwin Press is committed to improving education for all learners by publishing books and other professional development resources for those serving the field of PreK–12 education. By providing practical, hands-on materials, Corwin Press continues to carry out the promise of its motto: **"Helping Educators Do Their Work Better."**